THE MASTER'S TOUCH

The Master's Touch

True Stories of a Seventy's Ministry

By Mildred Nelson Smith

Copyright © 1973

HERALD PUBLISHING HOUSE
Independence, Missouri

All rights in this book are reserved. No part of the text may be reproduced in any form without written permission of the publishers, except brief quotations used in connection with reviews in magazines or newspapers.

Library of Congress Catalog Card No. 73-75883
ISBN 0-8309-0091-8

Printed in the United States of America

*To our children,
Alan, Ronald, Steven, Karen, and Douglas*

CONTENTS

The Calling of a Seventy 11
Direction at the Crossroads 17
Delbert's Accident 19
Called into the Kingdom 33
Sharing the Good News 40
A Communion Prayer 46
A Double Blessing 47
Wedding for Yvonne 50
Gene Makes His Covenant 57
New Shoes for Baby Gene 61
Fire! 63
Healing a Home 70
Co-creators with God 75
The Errant Doctor Bill 79
The Late Baptismal Service 82
On the Right Team 86
God's Messenger, the Mechanic 89
New Life for Marian 96
Treasured Memory 100
Witnessing to a "Witness" 103
Water Carrier or Son of God 107
Conrad Goes His Own Way 113
Agipito Could Never Forget 117
Unwarranted Garnishee 122
Tama, the Church, and the Kahuna 126
A Matter of Caring 131
The Uncertain Prostitute 135

A Time for Choosing	137
Mamasan's Magnificent Gift	140
Ami's Triumph	143
A Treasure Chest for Giving	148
Reconciliation	150
Bridge of Love	154
Taking God at His Word	158
Bonds Around the Globe	164
A Brave Woman	168
With Hands of Faith	172
Clara and the Big Wave	174
Ron Meets Daniel	180
A Message for the Women	183
The Seventy in Politics	188
The Substitute Sermon	192
Theories, Facts, and Faith	196
Lori's Missionary Funeral	198
A Young Man of Promise	202
The Fiery Furnace	204
Flight of Joy	209
No Funeral for Andy	211
The Impossible Border Crossing	214
Carmen, Child of Dignity	218
Carmen, Victim of Perfidy	227
Carmen, Mother of Elena	233
Mission of a Lemon Pie	238
Found in God's Good Time	241
Foiling the "Inspector"	243
A Telephone for the Guzmans	247
Andy the Mormon Priest	249
No Food in the House	257
Andy Never Quite Returns	262
All the Difference in the World	268

PREFACE

For more than two decades I have had the privilege of living with and working beside one who has been called and sent by God to lift men and women to the Christ for the Master's transforming touch. I have shared his joy when those to whom he has been called to minister have permitted him to lift them up. We have grieved together when, for some reason, his ministry apparently has not been effective. There have been times when I fear I have inadvertently interfered with his opportunity. There have been other times when I hope I have helped him discover and fulfill opportunities that he might otherwise never have known.

This book is not an effort to write my husband's biography, nor is it my own diary. Neither is it an attempt to chronicle all that he has done or even all that we have done together. Missing from it are many rich experiences with a myriad of people whom we love dearly and whose imprint on our lives waits to be told, if at all, at some future date.

In this volume you will find some glimpse into the life we have shared as we have tried to fulfill God's commission to us as a seventy's family, supported by the church so we can give full time to that ministry. Every story is based on an actual happening. Some names and locales have been changed to protect the privacy of individuals to whom the telling of the story might prove embarrassing. And in some cases I have taken liberty with the time and sequence of events.

I began telling stories of the ministry of the seventy at a time when I perceived that some people did not understand the nature of that ministry. It is my hope that these experiences may enrich the lives of many who desire to comprehend more fully the manner in which God moves among men.

My special thanks to my husband for sharing information with me which has made this book possible and to our son Alan who has read the manuscript and offered valuable assistance in its preparation.

M. N. S.

THE CALLING OF A SEVENTY

Delbert Smith entered the pavilion happily greeting other appointee ministers of the Reorganized Church of Jesus Christ of Latter Day Saints who had been called together by the apostle in charge of the area for a weekend of worship, study, and fellowship. It was a rare privilege to be under Apostle Oakman's tutelage, and my husband, who was then a young seventy, anticipated the forthcoming study expectantly.

It seemed to Delbert that the class had hardly started when he heard Brother Oakman saying, "If you will please stand, we will close the class with a prayer."

"Close the class? Why, he had just begun!" Del remonstrated silently and looked about him amazed that the others seemed ready for its ending. As the prayer proceeded, he gradually became aware of what had happened that had made him lose track of time.

As the class opened, Delbert had been abruptly removed from the beautiful Palos Park setting in which the group was meeting to an even more exquisite locale—a place of ethereal beauty. As in a dream he turned slowly, surveying all about him, trying to comprehend the wonder and splendor of his new environment. A pinpoint of light on the far horizon captured his attention; he stood transfixed, watching it intently. As he watched, the light began to grow steadily, increasing in size and intensity as though the source of it was advancing toward him. Awe and wonder swept over him as the light drew nearer, and he began to distinguish within it the form of a man. Hardly had the form appeared when to Delbert's mind it was identified as Jesus the Christ.

Suddenly he was overwhelmed by a deep sense of unworthiness. In one swift motion he ducked his head and threw up his arm to cover his face. Still the figure advanced, and Del felt the imprint of Christ's thought on his mind. Although no word was spoken, the seventy's attention was directed toward a large lump of bituminous coal that lay upon the ground.

"Pick it up!" came the command transmitted without words. Continuing to shield his face from the magnificent Presence he stooped to comply. Carefully he lifted the chunk of coal from the ground, and in response to yet another unspoken direction held it out toward the Divine One.

Delbert still did not dare to look at the Figure clothed in light. Instead, his gaze was focused on the coal in his hand as he extended it toward the Master. To his amazement he saw the finger of the Christ reach out and touch the coal, transforming it into the largest, most exquisite diamond Del had ever seen. Every facet glowed with the beauty of the reflected light of the Master. With reverence Del stood contemplating the transformation when Apostle Oakman's voice intruded with the announcement that the class was over.

For weeks Delbert pondered the experience, awed by its impact on him. He dared not speak of it lest he be misunderstood.

Then one night I received a telephone call intended for my husband. "Can you get a message to Delbert?" asked the caller when he found that the seventy was not in town.

"He probably hasn't had time to get to Albert Lea yet," I replied, "but I'm sure I can get him tonight."

"Then tell him he's got to come back over here." I knew

that "over here" was 110 miles away in another state for I recognized the caller as Ken Holloway, who had just been baptized that day in Minneapolis.

"What's the problem?" I inquired. Del had already gone a hundred miles in the opposite direction, and I knew he would want to know the reason for returning immediately to the area in which he had just been working.

"I have a man who wants to be baptized!" Ken spoke excitedly.

Ken and Mopsy had returned from their baptism to their home in the beautiful resort community surrounding Lake Chetek. Although Ken was still a breadwinner, many of their neighbors had retired to the leisurely life of fishing, boating, swimming, and golfing. Just across the way in a little cottage sheltered by stately oaks lived Jess and Marie Butcher. Jess was a retired bartender of no professed religion. Marie was a good Catholic. The Butchers and Holloways had been best friends since the Butchers had moved in.

When the Holloway car had slowed to a stop, Jess and Marie had emerged from their front door as though they had been keeping watch. As Ken struggled with his crutches in getting out of the car, Jess accosted him.

"Where the____ have you been all day?" Jess's rough greeting was friendly and concerned. He had kept a close eye on Ken since the accident and didn't want him doing anything that would delay his recovery.

"I've been to Minneapolis to be baptized," Ken announced happily. Had it been a few weeks earlier, he would have used even stronger expletives than Jess.

"Well, what do you know?" Jess mused. Then he continued, "That's something I've been thinking I ought to do—be baptized," he explained to make sure that Ken did not misunderstand.

"Come on in and let's talk about it," Ken said as he

adjusted his crutches and led the way across the drive to the house.

Pausing only to invite his guests to seat themselves, Ken swung himself across the room directly to the telephone and called Paul Harcourt, a priesthood member who lived nearby, to come and talk with Jess. When Paul left, Ken called for the seventy.

"Do you know what he did?" Ken asked. "He left without saying one word to Jess about baptizing him!"

I smiled a bit into the telephone. It was good to feel the enthusiasm of the newly baptized man. "Perhaps Paul feels that Jess should know a little more about the church before he gets all the way into it," I suggested gently.

"Then tell Del he has to get over here and teach him!" Ken was accustomed to having things done when they needed to be done.

"I'll have him call you tonight," I promised. "And Ken, it has been a wonderful day, hasn't it?" I reminded him, fearing that his disappointment that his friend's baptism was not arranged immediately might dim his memory of his own happy experience with the Christ.

"It has been wonderful!" Ken agreed thoughtfully.

Delbert called that night, then followed his call with a visit as soon as it could be arranged. Because Ken was still unable to move about freely, the meeting was arranged in the Holloway home.

"I know all about you ministers," Jess bragged, not at all the humble suppliant Del had thought he might find asking for baptism. "Why, I've talked to drunken Catholic priests, Protestant ministers, and Jewish rabbis." The seventy knew he was recalling his days behind the bar. "You don't fool me one bit!"

My husband wasn't quite sure whether Jess was being contemptuous or just issuing a challenge. Praying silently for direction the seventy replied patiently, "I'm not trying to fool you, Jess. Ken said you wanted to be baptized, and I think you ought to know what you're getting into before you take that step. I'd like to tell you about Christ and his church. Do you want me to, or don't you?" The seventy's voice was firm but he smiled as he spoke.

"Sure I want to hear," Jess said slowly, then glanced surreptitiously at Marie, wanting but not asking her approval of the arrangement.

It was nearly two o'clock the morning of the visit when I awakened with a start at the ringing of the telephone. "Mildred," Del was on the line, "I won't be home tonight. We've just stopped talking to have some lunch, and the Holloways have invited me to get some sleep here before I make the drive into the city."

Again and again it happened, the drive to Wisconsin for a cottage meeting, the late night call. Finally, Del just arranged to stay overnight each time he went to teach the Butchers.

"Jess thinks you're great!" Ken informed the seventy one night after Jess and Marie had gone home.

"He does?" Del asked in surprise. "He doesn't act like it! Why, I've never in my life seen a man fight so hard against the truth. He tries to tear down everything I say!" There was the tone of exasperation in my husband's voice.

"Yeah, but you ought to hear him quote you when you're gone," Ken said reassuringly.

After one particularly lively discussion that had gone on into the night, Marie suddenly announced, "I want to be baptized."

"You do?" Jess looked startled for a moment, then rushing across the room to Marie, he folded her in his arms. "Oh, Marie," he spoke tenderly and his voice quivered with the fervency of his emotion, "I have waited so long for you to say that!"

"You have?" It was the seventy's turn to be surprised and puzzled. "Then why have you been heckling me so?"

"Delbert, you know Marie is a Catholic. I have been asking all of the questions I thought she would need to have answered before she could decide to make the change," Jess explained earnestly. "You will baptize us, won't you?" In his earnestness Jess almost sounded afraid that Del would deny him that blessing. "I know that my life has been everything but saintly, but..."

The seventy didn't hear the rest. In that moment he stood again in the presence of the Christ, shielding his eyes from His radiance and holding out toward Him the lump of coal. Again he saw the finger of the Divine One touch the coal, and he wondered anew at the shimmering beauty of the diamond that sparkled in his hand.

With the imprint of the same Spirit by which the experience was first received, Delbert knew his mission as a seventy: to take humanity, however unrefined, and hold it humbly up to the Christ. That was the call of the seventy—to watch reverently as the touch of the Master's hand transformed life into a beautiful reflection of Himself in all His glory, intelligence, truth, and love. That was the joy of the seventy!

"Jess," the seventy said as he enfolded the man and his wife in his own long arms, "it will be the happiest moment of my life!" and his voice trembled with the wonder of it.

DIRECTION AT THE CROSSROADS

The day had been hot and frustrating. Even though it was nearly nine o'clock in the evening, the sun still shone across the vast prairie defying my husband's weariness. Saint-hunting could be a rewarding experience when there were Saints to be found, but some days they seemed to be nonexistent. Either they had moved from the address at which the statistician had last recorded them, or they had died, or they were just away. All day Delbert had driven across the rough gravel highways from one address to another only to be disappointed again and again. "Why won't the Saints practice the principle of the Gathering?" he wondered aloud. "At least then they could receive ministry regularly and the church would know when they died!"

As Del mused, he came to a crossroad and stopped. The one family the day of Saint-hunting had netted him had added one name to his list that the statistician did not have. A glance at the map showed the address to be thirty miles away in exactly the opposite direction of the hotel in which he had a room for the night. Should he make the effort? What if this, too, proved to be a dry haul? And if there were Saints there, would they welcome a guest at that time of night?

Without the facts by which to determine the wisest course, he prayed: "Lord, you used to give direction to your servants. I need direction now. Help me to choose the way that will bring ministry where it is needed."

Shifting the car into gear, Del headed toward Baker and

the Ganfield home. He covered the rough, dusty miles slowly as he drove toward the glow of the setting sun.

Suddenly it was dark except for scattered lights across the railroad tracks marking the presence of a small town. One lone person still on the street was able to provide directions to the home of the schoolteacher sought.

As he approached the Ganfield home he noticed a number of cars parked near the house. "Oh, no . . . not a party!" he said aloud. But he knocked anyway.

"Well, what do you want?" a woman asked from the doorway, an expression of annoyance on her otherwise kindly face.

"I am a minister of the Reorganized Church of Jesus Christ of Latter Day Saints and . . ."

"Come in, come in!" she said. The look of disapproval was quickly replaced by one of sheer relief. "Mother's in the other room. Come!" She spoke now as though he had been expected. Delbert followed her through the kitchen into the bedroom where other members of the family were gathered.

"Mother isn't expected to live through the night," Mrs. Ganfield said, explaining the presence of the rest of the family. Then turning to the sick woman she spoke distinctly. "Mother, this is Brother Smith."

"Oh. Then you did get our letter." The older woman spoke feebly.

"Letter?" Del questioned. "I know nothing about a letter." He was puzzled.

"We wrote to the district president four days ago asking for someone to come to administer to Mother. She has been so very ill."

"I haven't seen or heard from the district president for more than two weeks," my husband affirmed.

"Then God sent you!" The sick woman spoke reverently.

Delbert anointed the pale forehead with consecrated oil,

placed his hands gently on her head, and spoke to the Father-of-All about Sister Grice's need, of their thankfulness for the guidance that had brought him there, and of their faith in God's wisdom to grant the blessing needed by this household.

Del's heart sang as he retraced his route along the rough and dusty road, past the point of decision, and on to his hotel. Gradually the members of the family realized that death for their loved one was no longer near and dispersed to their own homes. Sister Grice lived on for many years, happily bearing her testimony of the healing she received the night God sent one of his servants to her door.

DELBERT'S ACCIDENT

I was far from our Minnesota home, over on the shores of Lake Michigan, when the unsettling telephone call came. It was the second evening of a rather unusual women's institute at which I was the guest speaker. The men had been invited to this session, and I sat with the women's leader on the front seat enjoying the prelude. The church was packed. Carefully the deacon opened the door beside the rostrum and beckoned me to join him.

"It's long distance for you," he whispered, hoping not to disturb the congregation. "Follow me.... I'll show you where the phone is."

Curiously I walked behind him to the cubbyhole in the basement where the telephone was hung on the wall.

"There's no need to be alarmed," the Minnesota District

president spoke reassuringly in response to my greeting. "Delbert has been in an accident, but he will be all right. We just thought you'd like to know before you come home."

"Where is he? How did it happen? Was there much damage to the car?" All of the usual questions were answered with reassurances that all was well and that there was no need to cut the institute short.

"When did it happen?" I questioned, trying hard not to give way to tears.

"Last night," Brother Elvin answered, "but don't worry about a thing. We'll meet you at the plane and tell you all about it tomorrow."

I hung up the receiver and began retracing my steps to the sanctuary. My mind was filled with questions I had not dared ask the district president. It had happened Monday. This was Tuesday night. Why did they wait so long to call? Delbert must have been hurt more than Brother Elvin admitted. They must have waited to see if he would survive before they called. The car was demolished. He would surely have been injured more than a little! Disturbing thoughts raced through my troubled mind. If only I could talk to someone! But I dared not say a word or I would cry, and I could not go before that church full of people with tear-filled eyes and a trembling voice. What I had to say was too important not to be said clearly. I couldn't disappoint all of those people who had made the effort to come, and copping out at this point wouldn't help Delbert in any way.

Breathing a prayer for my injured husband and for the blessing of calm for myself, I returned to the sanctuary. When the questioning eyes of the women's leader met mine I took a deep breath and whispered calmly, "Del had an accident," then turned to worship in the hymn that was being sung.

Beginning that talk was one of the most difficult tasks I

had ever performed. Once begun, however, I felt the warm assurance of the Spirit of God as I made the presentation. When I was finished, I joined the women's leader of the area in the reception line, still unable to speak of the disconcerting news I had received or of the fears it had fostered. Only once did tears nearly break through, and that was in gratitude when the stake bishop came through the line. He was returning from his own assignment for the evening and had not been in my audience.

"Things aren't as bad as you think," he whispered confidently as he gripped my hand.

"Thanks!" was all I could manage without tears. I wondered how he knew what had happened or that I was troubled.

"We can call off the rest of the institute," the women's leader volunteered when she had heard my story. "Maybe you should start home tonight."

In spite of my inclination to agree, I did want to fill my commitment. Women had come long distances for the meetings, which were to last through the morning and into the afternoon of the next day. A check of available travel accommodations soon made it apparent that to cancel the remainder of the meetings would be of no help. No train or bus or flight could get me home earlier.

"He may not know you," the nurse cautioned when I arrived at the hospital two days after the accident. "He has been insisting that he is not married."

"Not married!" I spoke more sharply than I had intended. I glanced at the rings which bore mute testimony of my relationship with my husband and remembered our son being cared for by Grandmother Thomas.

"Then he doesn't remember . . ."

"Sometimes he does." The nurse was kind. "When he first came in, he didn't even know his own name."

"Will he . . ." The question was never finished.

"We think the amnesia will be temporary, but don't expect too much," she cautioned.

"Amnesia." I pondered the word that I always before had associated with fiction. So that was why they didn't call for a whole day. "May I see him?" I asked, wondering what else I might not have been told.

Cautiously I approached the bed on which my husband lay sleeping. Only a small patch across his left temple gave evidence that he had been injured. I was so relieved to be with him and thankful to see him so nearly whole that I slipped quickly to his side, bent down, and kissed him gently on the cheek.

As soon as my lips touched him his whole body recoiled. In a flash he was half sitting, braced on his left arm, staring at me without recognition. His eyes were opened wide and glazed with terror. His pale face grimaced as he drew back against the wall, and his lips formed words that escaped only as guttural sounds. I drew back, fearful that I had done him irreparable harm.

"Your wife is here," the nurse announced as though Del would understand. Encouraged, I approached the bed again. "Don't you remember me, Del?"

Gradually the color returned to his blanched face, his body relaxed, and Delbert eased himself back onto his pillow. I reached out lovingly to assist him. As one in a dream, he wiped his hand across his eyes as though to clear away a fog that hovered there. "Mildred," he reached for my hand, "I'm glad you've come."

Bit by bit the story was pieced together. After Del had driven me to the plane that had taken me to my Michigan appointment, he had returned home to finish preparations for a wedding at which he was to officiate that evening in Wisconsin. The next thing he remembered, he was helping a highway patrolman place injured people in an ambulance.

"How about you?" The patrolman turned to my husband as the ambulance pulled away.

"Oh, I'm okay," Delbert responded confidently. "There's just a scratch on my head where it couldn't do much damage." He laughed as he daubed at the trickle of blood that was almost dry on his left temple.

"Hey!" The patrolman had been too busy with those who seemed severely injured to look at Del before. "You look a little green! Better sit down a moment anyway." He reached out solicitously to ease him into the patrol car seat. "Now where was it you were going?" he asked professionally.

The seventy hesitated. He brushed his hand across his face in a gesture that indicated an effort to think more clearly. Finally he answered bewilderedly, "I . . . I don't know. Where does this road go, anyway?"

"Say!" The patrolman headed for the driver's seat. "I think we'd better get you to the hospital, too!"

At the hospital Delbert insisted on walking to his room.

"Now let's see," the doctor started the examination. "What is your name?"

Del laughed heartily. "You'll have to tell me . . . then we'll both know." It was apparent that he was in shock.

"Can you tell us how to contact your wife?"

"Wife!" Delbert laughed. "Me married?" And he laughed again as if it were a great joke. "I'm not married," he affirmed emphatically. The doctor looked at his wedding band and continued the examination.

Delbert's identity and address were readily obtained from his billfold as were pictures of our son Alan and me. The hospital staff tried to contact me.

"Operator, the Smiths are not at home. May I take a message for them?" James Thomas answered our phone when he heard it ringing repeatedly.

"We are calling Mrs. Delbert Smith," the operator insisted.

"But she is not here. She is in Michigan. Can't I take the message?" Brother Thomas had become concerned when the call came for the third time.

Finally the connection was made and news of the accident transmitted. Immediately Brother Thomas called his son-in-law, who was also an elder, and in minutes they were on their way to the Forest City hospital to minister to Delbert.

For hours the hospital staff had been trying to stir up some spark of memory in my husband. He could reason expertly, but his memory for facts always stopped at the ambulance beside two wrecked cars. Because of the nature of his injury, the doctor had ordered that no sedative be given and that he not be allowed to sleep for a time. At one point he heard voices in the hall. Immediately he was alert. "That sounds like Brother Thomas," he informed the nurse. It was the first flicker of memory he had shown, and the delighted nurse went to bring in the men who were waiting to see him.

The visit was brief, and of course there was the ordinance of administration. No sooner had the men left the room than Del rang the bell for the nurse.

"Who were those men?" he asked, and it was evident that he was genuinely puzzled. "It seems I should know them, but I can't remember who they are."

Bedtime came, and Delbert was very tired. "The doctor says I can give you a sleeping pill now," the nurse said.

"Sleeping pill!" Del responded with just a hint of indignation in his voice. "What do I need a sleeping pill for? Just you get out of here and give me a chance," he insisted. "I'll sleep."

Delbert wakened with the morning and lay trying to remember. Vaguely he recalled the feel of hands on his head and the administrative prayer. The memory had a dreamlike quality but he was certain someone had been near him who had anointed him with oil, placed hands on his head, and prayed for him.

"Know where you are?" the nurse questioned cheerfully when she saw him stir.

"I must be in a hospital." Del studied his hospital gown intently.

"Do you know why you are here?" the nurse was testing to see if his memory of the accident had survived his sleep.

"There was an accident . . ." his hesitating statement was almost a question.

"A car accident," the nurse prompted, "on Highway 14. Do you know where you were going?" The nurse had been instructed by the doctor to try to help my husband recall events that preceded the accident.

"I just . . . can't . . . remember." He shook his head in discouragement.

"Could you have been going to a wedding?" The nurse left the room on an errand.

"A wedding . . . a wedding . . . a wedding . . ." The thought seemed to have some credence. "If I was going to a wedding," Del reasoned, "there should be some notes in my coat pocket."

Cautiously he slipped from his bed and went to the closet. Sure enough, in his pocket he found the notes.

* * * *

At Chetek the little church was filled to overflowing with guests. Since there was only a piano and Donna wanted organ music for her prelude, a recording had been brought for the occasion. When the time for the service arrived, the record was started while the wedding party waited anxiously for the minister's arrival. When the prelude was finished and Delbert had not arrived it was begun again. Repeatedly the record was played—but still no Delbert. Finally the district president was called from among the guests.

"We don't know what has happened to Brother Smith," the bride-to-be was almost in tears. "Do you suppose he forgot?"

"Oh, no!" Brother Elvin assured them. "He was getting ready to come when we left, and we ate supper on the way. He even asked to ride with us, but we were going to the lake afterward, and he had to get back home."

"Could you marry us?" Donna knew Wesley was well qualified and experienced in this phase of his ministry. "We can't keep the guests waiting much longer," the bride was apologetic.

"Just give me a minute to get the Scriptures," he responded reassuringly. The marriage was solemnized without Delbert or any explanation of his absence.

Without waiting for the reception, Wesley rushed to the Atwood house and telephoned. By then the Thomases had word of the accident, and Wesley and Jay arrived at the hospital in time for Wesley's hands to be among those that touched Delbert's head as supplication was made to heaven in his behalf.

"Now look here, young lady. Nobody is going to rush me!" the doctor spoke brusquely. "I've had too much experience with head injuries in the South Pacific not to know how dangerous they are."

"I'm not trying to rush you," I explained. "It's just that my husband is scheduled at a family camp next week, and we need to get someone to replace him if he cannot go."

"How do I know whether he'll be able to go or not?" The doctor appeared angry. "I'm no prophet! Here he barely knows who he is, and you want me to turn him loose!"

"I'm sorry." I felt the tears welling up in my eyes and distorting my voice. I always was plagued by too-ready tears when I wanted most to be calm. "I don't want you to dismiss him until he's ready. I just want to know how to plan." I finished lamely feeling like a frightened child who had just been scolded unjustly.

"Well, don't!" The doctor was obviously closing the interview. "I'll dismiss him when he's ready to leave."

Delbert was dismissed on Wednesday. "He has made history here," the one who settled the hospital bill with me observed. "He's the first patient ever to remain overnight in this hospital and leave without a single medication. Not one pill," she emphasized, "has he had in more than a week!"

"I'm glad!" I said simply, and silently offered a prayer of thanksgiving.

Delbert had explained the need for his services at the camp. "If you'll do nothing but sit in the shade and drink pink lemonade," the doctor had asserted, "you may go. Understand, though. You're not to do a thing!"

Our family arrived at the camp on the heels of a storm. High winds had uprooted a huge tree that had shaded the play area near the big house that served as a dorm, kitchen, dining hall, and meeting rooms for the small band of Saints who rented the facility from the local 4-H organization early each summer. The deluge of water that had been dumped from the clouds seemed to have dampened the spirits of those attending the camp. The young people seemed particularly disheartened.

Delbert could stand such an atmosphere for only minutes. Hardly had our belongings been deposited in the quarters assigned to the seventy's family than he found a ball and was challenging the youth to a game of dodge ball. It wasn't until his right pant leg began to feel tight that he remembered the doctor's instruction. Looking down he saw his knee swollen until it looked like a balloon. Del had not realized that his knee had been injured until it began to swell. Now he recalled seeing the control knobs on the dash flattened and realized it must have been his knee that had hit them.

Friday morning found my husband deeply involved in the operation of the camp. It had been necessary for the apostle and another seventy who had been at camp to leave and the staff was shorthanded. He had helped the patriarch conduct the prayer service and now stood facing a class of eager young people. "I really have no lesson prepared," he confided. "I know that many of you come from areas isolated from the church. Do you have any questions you would like to ask about Christ's church or your part in it?"

The questions seemed to center on the gifts of the Spirit of God—prophecy, healing, tongues ... ministries they had heard about but many had never experienced. Of these, tongues seemed to concern the youth most. How anyone could speak in a language he did not know was beyond their comprehension and almost out of the realm of credibility.

Delbert tried to explain that God speaks all languages and by the imprint of his Spirit on the mind of the willing and spiritually alert can help them use languages they do not know to minister to those who have need. He emphasized that the genuine gift of tongues from God is never just a hodgepodge of syllables but a real language that can be understood by those who know it. He assured them that when God grants the gift as a manifestation of his Spirit, someone does understand it or it is interpreted into the language of the congregation so the people there can benefit by such ministry.

He had them read with him the fourteenth chapter of I Corinthians (Apostle Paul's instruction concerning the nature and use of the gift) and chapter twelve (Paul's discussion of it as a manifestation of the Spirit of God).

"The gifts of the Spirit should not be rare events in Christ's church," the seventy told them earnestly. "If the Spirit of God is at work among the Saints, that Spirit will be manifest in ministry."

Still it did not seem real to the young listeners. Perhaps testimonies of people he knew and his own testimony would be more meaningful. Without any difficulty associated with his amnesia, he recalled in vivid detail the testimonies that were meaningful to him.

First he told the class of the time a young Japanese attended a Conference prayer meeting in the basement of the old Stone Church in Independence, Missouri. One of the ministers arose and addressed the "keike Kapanee" present. The young oriental, who was not at that time a member of the Church of Jesus Christ, perked up quickly and gave full attention, for that was the Hawaiian term for "little" or "young Japanese." Hastily he surveyed the congregation. Obviously the minister was speaking to him, for he was the only "keike Kapanee" present. Then there followed, in what he recognized as perfect Japanese, a message from God assuring him that he had been directed to this church and was someday to minister in it. The message did not need to be interpreted, for the one for whom it was intended knew the language in which it was given and understood perfectly.

In later years this man bore his testimony as an elder in Christ's church of the value of the experience to him. His mother was a Buddhist faith healer and performed marvelous acts of healing. Seeing such miracles, the young Japanese would sometimes wonder where God's truth really lay—in the Buddhist faith of his mother or in the Christian faith to which he had given his allegiance. Always there would come the memory of the message from God, given in Japanese, by a man who did not know the language, assuring him that God had called him into His truth to minister for Him among his people.

Delbert told the class how, as a graduate student at Iowa State College (later Iowa State University), he had presided over the congregation and how he and I had been concerned that many of the church member students had never experienced the gifts of prophecy or tongues. They were hampered in their efforts to share the gospel with their friends because of the lack of a personal testimony to share convincingly the knowledge that God is alive and active in the affairs of men. So he and I had made it a matter of fasting and prayer. At the reunion that summer when several of the students were present, the congregation sat for nearly an hour and three quarters receiving almost continual prophecy, tongues, and the interpretation of tongues. Seven different men of the priesthood had ministered using these gifts. The students had their own testimony to share.

He told my experience as a young woman at the Pawnee, Oklahoma, reunion. It was the year that another young seventy and his wife had returned to the States from Tahiti for the birth of their first child.

At a morning prayer service an evangelist-patriarch arose to speak. Before he said a word, I knew by the Spirit of God that he would speak in tongues and that the young seventy would understand. I was so certain of it that words coming in a language I did not understand were no surprise to me, even though I was aware that the patriarch knew only English. I really expected that the seventy would interpret the message for him. However, when the patriarch finished speaking in the tongue that I did not understand, he immediately began interpreting the message in English. As he spoke, he turned from one person or couple to another gesturing as he had when he first spoke. I thought, "The seventy will confirm that the tongue is genuine, for I know he understood it."

But when the patriarch sat down, the seventy's wife arose and began to bear her testimony, making no reference to the language of the gift just received by the congregation. I was so surprised that I turned around to see why the seventy had not spoken. There he sat so completely overcome with emotion that he could not speak, so his wife—sensitive to his need—had borne her testimony of God's love to give him a chance to regain control of himself.

When he spoke, the seventy from Tahiti began, "I believe this gift was given not so much to bless this people as to bless a people seven thousand miles away." Then he explained that the patriarch had spoken that morning in the dialect of a group of South Sea Island Saints isolated from ministry for more than seven years before he visited them. He was able to stay with them for just a bit over two weeks, and since his return to the States he had been trying to write something to them that would encourage them. Everything he wrote seemed totally inadequate. "But now," he affirmed, "I can tell them that I heard this message from God in their tongue, spoken by a man who did not know their language, and it will bless them."

Among the testimonies that followed was the testimony of the wife of another seventy who had been asked to go to England on a mission. It was soon after World War II, and life was difficult in England. Food and clothing were hard to get, and fuel was not in adequate supply. So, she said, she had gone to the woods beside the camp that morning and had talked to the Lord about it. She had told him that if it was really He who wanted them to go, she was willing. But if it was not, she wanted another assignment. She asked him to let her know that morning in tongues. Her affirmative answer was among the messages delivered through the gift of tongues and their interpretation.

After the service was finished, many gathered at the front of the tabernacle. The patriarch would ask the seventy from Tahiti, "When I said – – – – – in English, how did I say it?" and the younger man would reply in the Polynesian tongue.

"It was a great experience for Mildred," Del finished. But he could see that there was still minimal understanding.

"It's just as clear as mud," Del empathized with his young listeners, "isn't it? You're like those students at Ames. You need your own testimony, don't you?" There was nodded agreement. "Well, let me tell you, you have every right to that testimony. If you really want to be better witnesses for Christ, why don't you ask God for such an experience?"

Saturday morning the youth group sat expectantly in the east room of the L-shaped meeting area. Walls had been removed to make open space between what had once been the living room and the dining room of the old house. By using the area at the apex of the L for pulpit and priesthood, the minister could speak to the people in both rooms, and all could participate in one service.

As the prayer meeting got under way, the presence of the Spirit of God was readily felt. Finally the patriarch, who was not aware of the prayer of the youth, arose and, turning to the youth group, began speaking in tongues. With the interpretation there came commendation for their desires and questing, encouragement and instruction for the future, personal ministry to some, and a blessing to all. There was a benedictory prayer, and Del strode directly to the section occupied by his class.

"Now do you know what I mean?" There was really no reason to question. Radiant faces bore eloquent testimony of the impact of the God-given ministry, and affirmative nods spilled tears of joy from their eyes.

CALLED INTO THE KINGDOM

"Delbert," I settled into my seat beside my husband as we pulled away from the new farmstead we had been visiting, "there is your first elder on the Mesabe Iron Range."

"I don't think he thinks so," Del smiled back. "I'm not sure he even likes us very much at this moment."

"Nevertheless," I insisted, "he will be the first elder of Christ's church ordained up here."

"He has certainly had experience with the Spirit of God. If he keeps responding to that Spirit, I'm sure God will have a great work for him to do," Del agreed, "and we surely need someone up here on the range to shepherd the flock."

"I want you to meet this Harvey Seeley," Nellie Longmore had announced excitedly when the seventy had arrived to work for a few weeks in the northern Minnesota area. "I have invited him to sing at the services Sunday so you can meet him."

The Longmore living quarters back of the family café in the rustic mining town of Bovey provided the center of activities for the Saints on the Iron Range. Christ and his way were often the topic of conversation in the café, too, if Sister Longmore spotted someone who seemed to have a special need or particular potential . . . or just someone who would listen to her favorite topic of conversation. The rough miners who daily joined her husband in the pits seemed never to mind. Anyone who could cook and put up lunches like Nellie Longmore could say anything she liked while they ate.

Extra activity in the church he regularly attended kept

Harvey from appearing at the afternoon meeting to sing. Assured by Sister Longmore that Harvey really did want to meet Delbert we went to the Seeley farm the next day. There was no telephone in the area, so we had no choice but to arrive unannounced.

Set in a clearing beside a rough country lane the new farmstead was beginning to take shape. Stumps bright with new wood dotted the entire clearing, witnessing the recency with which the area had still been virgin forest. The shell of the house stood complete—so new that the siding matched the brightness of the stumps, and labels were still sticking to the window glass. Behind the house a rough pole corral confined a cow, a pig, and a pony. A crude sled held a barrel of water brought from a neighbor's well, and the tall electric poles that followed the trail from the main road found their terminus at the house.

Margery was doing the laundry when we arrived. The ringer washer and the tubs were set on a temporary platform just outside the backdoor near the water barrel. An ingenious electrical device for warming the water dangled from a bent nail under the eaves. Until there was a well with a water system and plumbing, the substitute served admirably. Inside the house Harvey worked to complete the structure.

"I am Delbert Smith. This is my wife, Mildred, and our son Alan," Del introduced his family when the slight dark-haired man appeared in the doorway in response to his wife's call. "Nellie Longmore sent us. We were sorry you could not make it to the meeting yesterday."

"Oh, yes!" Harvey was cordial. "You're the new preacher who is going to hold services at the Longmores for a while. I've heard about you. Won't you come in?"

"I'll just help your wife finish this laundry," I volunteered, "while you fellows talk. We certainly don't want the water to get cold."

Margery protested but then accepted my offer.

"You go ahead with your work, too," Delbert insisted. "We can get acquainted while you work."

With two at work on the laundry, the clothes were soon on the line and the women joined the men inside the house.

"Nellie keeps telling me your church is different from the rest of us Protestants," Harvey introduced the subject that he knew the seventy had come to discuss with him. "I've been saved for many years now. What more can you offer me than salvation?" Harvey was certain there was no answer to that question, so without waiting for one he questioned the seventy abruptly, "Are you saved?"

"If I keep on as I am now, I hope to be saved," Del answered simply.

"Well, I *know* I'm saved!" Harvey was positive in his declaration, but Delbert's reply bothered him. He looked quizzically at the seventy for a moment trying to figure out why one who had dedicated his life to Christ as this minister evidently had would not be as certain of salvation as he.

Seeing his puzzlement, Del added, "You know the Scriptures say it is he that endures to the end who is saved. Actually, I think our problem in understanding each other is largely one of semantics. When I say 'saved' I mean something associated with the final great judgment day. When you say 'saved' I think you mean an experience with God that changed your life. We would call it a conversion experience, and such an experience does offer saving power. Is that what you mean?"

"Maybe so," Harvey answered thoughtfully.

"I have had many rich experiences with God, though, that have changed my life and given me power to become more like the Christ," the seventy testified. "And we have experienced in great abundance the gifts of the Spirit that Christ said should follow those who believe."

"Do you speak in tongues?" This was the gift of the Spirit Harvey's denomination stressed as evidence that one really did have the Holy Ghost.

"No," Del admitted, "I have never spoken in tongues. That has not been my gift. You know, Harvey, God gives gifts to people as he wills, and not all have the same gift. You know how Paul explains it in I Corinthians, chapter twelve: 'Are all apostles? Are all prophets? Are all teachers? Are all workers of miracles? Have all the gifts of healing? Do all speak with tongues? Do all interpret? I say unto you, Nay; for I have shown unto you a more excellent way.'"

"I have been ministered to by the gift of tongues," Del continued, "as they have been spoken by others. Mildred, too, has received such ministry. Mildred, will you tell the Seeleys about the tongue you heard when one who spoke Tahitian was there and understood it?" I told the story.

"You know, one of our friends had an experience like that," Harvey was eager to share his testimony. "He went out to the barn to pray one day and he prayed in tongues. His Norwegian hired hand heard him and understood the prayer in Norwegian. My friend knew only the English language."

"Isn't it marvelous that God has the power to use all languages to bless men in need?" Delbert spoke appreciatively of Harvey's testimony. "I don't understand how he does it, but I do know that in the genuine gift of tongues he uses real languages and not meaningless syllables. And, of course, there is always the interpretation that accompanies the tongue—unless, of course, it is in a language understood by the people to whom it is directed."

"Is it always that way in your church?" Harvey was wistfully skeptical.

"Always!" Delbert answered reassuringly.

The conversation touched on other gifts of the Spirit enumerated by Paul, and always both men had a testimony.

The conversations became frequent and spirited. Del was certain that Harvey was responding to the larger truth he had come to share. Harvey wasn't so certain. He was hearing strange things about modern prophets, American Scriptures, authoritative priesthood. They didn't quite fit into the picture for a solid Bible Christian who knew he was saved. Harvey's long experience in responding to the Spirit of God, however, led him to continue to ask for that Spirit's direction.

Three times Harvey dreamed strange dreams. Once he dreamed that he lay in his bed in the unfinished upstairs bedroom of their new house. Hanging from a beam there was a large splinter still attached to the beam by heavy wood fibers. In his dream, Harvey was praying. "Father," he said, "if Brother Smith is telling me the truth and he really does represent your church, please cause that splinter to fall." Without a moment's hesitation the splinter plummeted to the floor.

A second time he dreamed that a friend with whom he had discussed his need for a rabbit hutch had brought him one to work the next day. Harvey awoke thinking that it was strange he should dream about the hutch and determined to see his friend about it as soon as he got to work. They were on their way to the pit when Harvey's friend hailed him. "Say, Harvey, I have something for you in the truck."

"The rabbit hutch?" Harvey questioned.

"Sure thing," responded his friend.

M-m-m, thought Harvey. What a strange coincidence! Aloud he called back, "Good! I'll look it over at noon."

Harvey was a member of a car pool providing transportation to work. In Harvey's third dream, he and the other members of the pool were riding to work in a car that did not belong in the pool. The morning after the dream, the driver assigned for the day arrived on schedule. Only a short way down the road, however, there was trouble. The transmission went out of the car. The driver was walking toward a nearby house to phone another member of the pool to come for them when Harvey spotted the red car he had seen in his dream coming down the road. "Never mind, Bud," he yelled to his departing companion. "Here comes our ride."

Moments later the car of his dream arrived on the scene, picked up the stranded passengers from the disabled car, and took them all to work. Harvey didn't join in the jovial banter on the way. His mind was seriously occupied. The last two of his dreams had come true in meticulous detail. Could it be possible that the Lord was trying to tell him that the first one was likewise valid?

The date was set for a baptismal service. Several children and youth were to be baptized into the Restoration faith. The seventy invited Harvey and Marge to make their larger covenant with God at that service.

"I don't know, Delbert," Harvey responded uncertainly. "It sounds good, but before I leave my church, I have to be certain. Is Brother Day going to be here for the service?" Harvey referred to an old-time missionary who frequently came from his home in Bemiji to minister to the little group of nonresident Saints who met at the Longmore home. Because of him and Nellie, Del's message had not been entirely new. And he and Del had ministered together on occasions in which they could both be in the area during the many months since Del's first call at the Seeley farm.

"No," Del replied regretfully. "I asked him to be here to help with the service, but he wrote back saying it would be impossible for him to come."

"Marge," Harvey confided when Del was gone, "I don't want to make a mistake. I have prayed that Brother Day will come for the service. If he comes it will be my assurance that I am to be baptized."

All day Saturday Harvey listened for the distinctive sound of Brother Day's ancient Ford wheezing up the lane—uncertain that he wanted Brother Day to come, for he knew that if the minister did appear he and his family would start a new life on Sunday.

Late Saturday evening the Seeleys decided to drive out to visit Marge's family. As they drove through Grand Rapids on their way, Harvey suggested, "Maybe we had better stop and call to see if Mother needs anything from town."

"Where will we find a phone?" Marge questioned.

Harvey thought a moment. "There'll be one in the bus depot, won't there? Let's stop there."

As Harvey entered the depot from the front door in search of a telephone, the passengers arriving from Bemiji entered from the platform door.

"Harvey!" A familiar voice rang out above the noise of shuffling feet and babbling conversation.

Startled, Harvey searched the group. "Brother Day! Brother Day!" He repeated the elder's name again as he spotted the old man coming out of the crowd toward him.

"I hear there's a baptismal service tomorrow," Brother Day smiled happily. "Are you going to be baptized, Harvey?"

"I wasn't going to be," Harvey's voice reflected the awe which he felt at what was happening. "But I am now!" he added, shaking the elderly man's hand firmly.

SHARING THE GOOD NEWS

"Can't you see?" Harvey stood, Bible in hand, pleading earnestly with the Brayfords to understand what he and Marge had found in the Restoration faith when Delbert and I arrived at the open door of Marge's parents' home. It was the night of Harvey's baptismal day. The service of confirmation had been barely finished when he said to Del, "I'm going to Mother's. She's a dedicated Christian. She has to know about this! Will you come, too?"

"You go on over," my husband suggested. "We'll come as soon as I finish up here."

When we arrived, however, things seemed not to be going as the enthusiastic new member had hoped.

"Brother Smith," Harvey turned to the seventy, discouragement beginning to cloud his countenance, "it's so plain. Why can't she see it?"

"Harvey," Del smiled warmly, "if I remember correctly, you didn't see it the first time any of us talked to you about it either. Remember that first day we visited you? You put up a lot of resistance. Remember?"

"Yeah!" Harvey conceded and laughed with relief at the memory. "I didn't think that day I'd ever be trying to convince Marge's mother that you were right!"

"Give the Brayfords a little time to study it out for themselves," Delbert counseled, "and to get their own testimony from the Father as you did."

"I've been gloriously saved!" Mrs. Brayford explained when we had been properly admitted to the house and introduced to the family. "You can't imagine what a sinner I was before Jesus came into my life. I don't see what you can offer me more than salvation!"

Del glanced at Harvey, wondering if he recognized the familiar statement as a duplicate of his own of a few months ago. Before he could comment, Harvey was speaking eagerly again.

"I was saved, too. You know that, Mother. But this is different. It's like stepping with Christ into a whole new world. Everything is different now. In Christ's church it's not your own salvation that you're concerned about any more. Instead, you know that with him you're going to help build a whole new world. It's for his kingdom's sake that you dedicate your life!" There was no mistaking the young man's sincerity. The Brayfords listened respectfully to their son-in-law, but it was clear that they did not comprehend.

"Maybe you'd like for us to come over and show you some slides and tell you more about it," Delbert suggested.

The Brayfords nodded assent. They did respect their son-in-law, and they knew he had experienced something beyond his own "salvation" that had made him a new man.

Night after night Harvey and Marge, Del and I visited the rural home of the Brayfords. Like many other residents of the area, Carl Brayford worked in the iron mines for a living. On the side, the family raised a little corn and hay for their cow and pigs and garden stuff for their family on their miniature farm cleared from the wilderness. While our children played or slept in the bedroom side by side crosswise on the bed to make room for them all, we adults shared the message of the Restoration.

* * * * *

One beautiful fall evening we hurried back from visiting the Saints in the vicinity of Virginia and Hibbing to share again with the Brayfords. We laughed as we recalled the experience of the early morning. Just outside of town when we started our trip, we had passed two hitchhikers on the road. "Those are Mormon elders!" I had spotted the books under their arms. That, added to the neat suits and distinctive straw hats on two clean-cut young men, convinced me I could not be mistaken. "Let's go back and pick them up," I suggested.

Agreeably, Del turned around in the road and returned for the elders. When they learned that we were members of the Reorganized Church of Jesus Christ of Latter Day Saints, they shared their latest bit of news of the Reorganization.

"One of your important patriarchs has just moved to Minneapolis," they declared. "One of Joseph Smith's progeny!"

"Oh?" Del questioned. "I didn't know that!"

"Oh, yes!" The eager young men were glad to be able to inform us of such an important event in our church. "His name is Elbert Smith."

"No." I laughed as I turned toward the back seat to converse with the elders. "I'm afraid someone has misinformed you. Our name is Smith, and Delbert is a seventy in the Reorganized Church of Jesus Christ. He's the only one of the church's official family who has moved to Minneapolis in the last two years."

"Oh, no!" the elders insisted. "Elbert Smith, your presiding patriarch, has moved there. We know!"

"I don't mind being confused with Brother Elbert," Delbert shrugged and they let the subject drop.

* * * * *

The trip from Virginia to Grand Rapids had always fascinated us. In summer there were the deep rich greens of forests and fields set with sparkling lakes in unexpected places. In fall, the forests became vistas of radiant reds, yellows, oranges, and browns touched here and there with the soft green of pines and the bluegreen of fir trees. Huge piles of taconite waited beside open pits to be transported to the smelters where newly discovered processing methods made the utilization of the low-grade ore profitable. And always there were the enormous open pits like terraced mountainsides carved into the earth. These were perpetually clothed in fall colors because of the oxidation of the iron.

The mines were always alive with motion. Ant-like figures scurried to and fro. We knew the crawling things were actually huge Caterpillar tractors, mammoth digging cranes with shovels lifting prodigious loads, lumbering transport trucks, and even railroad cars and engines that would carry the ore to Duluth to be shipped on barges to smelters across the lake and around the world. The tiny specks that moved about were men. We knew without seeing them that they were red with dust. Standing on the edge of such a spectacular man-made imprint on the face of the earth or just observing it as we passed never failed to spark in us a deep sense of reverence for the handiwork of God and the craftsmanship of man.

This evening there was a special request from Curtis Brayford, Marge's brother. Curtis was an epileptic. His efforts to work were always plagued by the danger of his having a seizure at a moment when such an event would be disastrous to him and to others. "I feel so worthless," Curtis confided. "Do you think God could heal me so I can work like a man?"

"I know God loves you," the seventy affirmed, "and I know he can heal you. Whether he will I cannot promise. Remember Paul? He asked three times for the Lord to remove the thorn in his flesh, and the Lord helped him to understand that it was better for him to continue to carry the thorn. We will unite our faith, Curtis, and we'll ask him."

At the close of the evening's presentation of the gospel message, Curtis was anointed with oil, and with rare eloquence Delbert petitioned the Father for His blessing.

It was the night that Del presented the Book of Mormon that proved to be an especially significant one in the life of the Brayfords. "You see," the seventy spoke earnestly in conclusion, "God knew that there would come a day when learned men would say that Jesus was just a good man, a prophet, teacher, a historical figure about whom myths cast an aura of divinity. For that day he preserved a record of a second branch of the house of Israel to come forth 'out of the dust' as a 'sealed book' bearing 'the revelation of God' as Isaiah proclaimed, speaking as one with whom the people are familiar because its message is so like that of the Bible record which they already know. The words of the record are delivered to one who is learned who declares he cannot read a sealed book, but the book is read by one who is not learned by the gift and power of God. It is to come forth a little while before Lebanon again becomes 'a fruitful field ... esteemed as a forest' and in a day when the deaf may hear and the blind may read its words. This record is to be joined with the record of Judah, which we know as the Bible, in the last days, according to the prophet Ezekiel, to bear unmistakable testimony of Jesus as the Christ, the living Son of God. The Book of Mormon puts it this way: '... to the convincing of the Jew and Gentile that Jesus is the Christ.' This day has come. Lebanon is again a fruitful field esteemed as a forest. The blind do read and the deaf do hear despite their handicaps. Learned men do misrepresent the Christ, and here is a second testimony of him—the record of Joseph of which Ezekiel spoke, bearing witness that he did arise from the dead, that he did minister to his people in the Americas, that he continues to live and minister wherever men are found endeavoring to establish his kingdom firmly upon the earth."

"Brother Smith," Gladys Brayford's voice trembled with emotion as she addressed the seventy, "I thought I had given my life entirely to my Lord when I was saved. Now I see how little I really understood! I know I don't understand it all yet, but I'm ready now to dedicate my life to building his kingdom if you'll baptize me."

"You know I'll baptize you!" Delbert responded joyfully.

"Do you suppose He'd have a place to use an old codger like me?" Carl Brayford's voice, too, showed a trace of the tears he had retreated to the kitchen to conceal.

"Carl!" Gladys' cry of surprise rang out as she rushed across the room into her husband's arms, "I didn't think you ... Well, you know ... you never were saved ... you didn't think much about church. ... I just never thought ..." The happy woman, stammering hopelessly, embraced her husband with delight.

"Yeah!" Carl agreed brusquely. "But it's like you said. This is different. If there's a kingdom to build I want in on it."

Curtis joined his decision with that of his parents.

"Even if God does not heal you?" Del wanted no illusions, no unjustified hopes to influence Curtis's decision to be baptized.

"You asked for His will to be done, didn't you? I'll trust Him!" he said resolutely.

A COMMUNION PRAYER

With the addition of the Brayfords, the Seeleys, and others to the little group of Saints and the reactivation of members scattered over the range, the Longmore home became too small to accommodate services, so the congregation moved into a hall . . . and God moved to provide for the shepherding of the flock. Now these people could experience the ordinances of the church without waiting for the seventy, Brother Day, Brother Thomas, or any minister from another congregation more adequately supplied with priesthood. Visiting ministers did continue to come, however, to assist.

"Do you know what happened?" Nellie Longmore was distressed when the seventy was once more on the Iron Range for ministry. "Last Communion Sunday Harvey left the Communion prayers at home, so he made up his own! I didn't know what to do!" The woman's voice had taken on an element of horrified incredulity. "I spoke to him about it, but he didn't seem to think it was important."

"Nellie," Del said as he gave the distraught woman an affectionate pat on the back, "you've had the responsibility of the work up here for so long that you just can't relax, can you? Come. Tell me about those prayers. Were they good ones?"

"Now Delbert Smith, don't you josh with me!" Nellie had relaxed since sharing her concern.

"You do believe that God can reveal himself to men, don't you?" My husband became more serious, for he did understand the good woman's anxiety.

"Absolutely, Delbert. You know I do." Nellie was a bit hurt that anyone would question her belief in revelation.

"And you really believe that he hears and answers the prayers of the righteous, don't you?" Del was persistent.

"I really believe he does!" Nellie affirmed.

"Then if you talk to God about it, I'm sure he'll find a way to get through to Harvey." The seventy's inference that her prayers should qualify as efficacious ameliorated the hurt she had felt earlier.

"Just remember, Nellie," Del continued, "Harvey has been an elder for only a few weeks, and he's had to learn on his own. He's our first elder on the Iron Range, so there has been no one for him even to observe. How about it? Let's let him make a mistake or two and pray for him and help him all we can. Okay?"

Nellie nodded. "Our first elder on the Iron Range!" she repeated the words thankfully. "After all these years of waiting!"

A DOUBLE BLESSING

The pungent farmyard odor gave way to the fragrance of the evening meal as we entered the Hendersons' Canadian farm home. Quickly the Henderson children whisked Alan and Ron away to see a baby colt, and I joined Mrs. Henderson in the kitchen to complete dinner preparations. The men settled in the comfortable living room to talk.

"Things must be going well for you, Brother Tom," Delbert observed remembering the well-kept appearance of the house, the happy faces of the children, and tantalizing smell coming from the kitchen.

"No, Brother Smith." The robust appearing farmer shook his head gravely. "Things are not going well. It's no longer possible for me to make a living for my family out here on the farm."

"You do have another job, don't you?" Del was sure Tom had a job in town.

Again the man's head indicated a negative answer, but he spoke affirmatively. "Yes, for a while I have. My legs are getting so bad, though, that I'm not going to be able to keep it very long. You can't imagine the pain!"

"Have you seen a doctor?" Del inquired solicitously.

"The doctor has done all he can, and they just get worse." There could be no doubt that the man was discouraged.

There was a long pause as the seventy walked to the window and surveyed the rough land littered with rocks and plagued by scrub brush in the area beyond the pasture in front of him. It was little wonder that Tom could not care for his growing family on the thin land. Del's heart went out to the man sitting in the chair behind him. "Oh, God, how can I help?" he questioned silently.

"Brother Smith," there was hesitant hope in Tom Henderson's voice as he addressed the seventy, "would you and Brother Thomas administer to me? If I just had my legs back, I know I could provide for my family." He paused a moment as if gathering courage to express his hope. "And I'm sure God can give them back to me!"

"Can you wait until after church tomorrow?" Delbert felt that would be an appropriate time to approach the Father in such an important request. "We will fast and pray tomorrow morning and have the ordinance of administration right after the service. How does that sound to you?"

Tom agreed.

*****

The preaching ended, and most of the congregation gathered for the usual Sunday socializing on the front steps of the old home that had been converted into a church. Tom Henderson hobbled painfully to a chair that Del had placed at the front of the chapel. I had shared in Del and Brother Thomas's concern and their fasting and prayer that morning and now sat on a chair in the front row of the chapel seats near the place of administration. As the hands of the seventy and the patriarch touched the head of the suffering farmer, the Spirit of God engulfed them and reached out to me.

For a long time I had been plagued with a persistently irritating illness. I had kept hoping that medication would relieve my discomfort and had never even thought of asking the elders to lay their hands on my head and petition for its removal. There had been times when I had suffered most that I had asked God's direction and help in finding relief.

Now as Tom Henderson received administration, I felt as if I were being lifted from my chair. Distinctly I felt the imprint of a hand as it passed over the afflicted part of my body, and I knew that healing had come.

As the elders prayed, Tom, too, felt the powerful spirit of healing. The pain drained from his legs, and he arose, with thankful tears streaming down his cheeks, and walked from the church. Tomorrow he would continue making a living for his family.

WEDDING FOR YVONNE

"Oh, Yvonne," Gene Tardy beamed with happiness as he drew his fianceé to him in an affectionate embrace, "ours is going to be the most beautiful wedding there has ever been on the Iron Range!"

I turned sideways in the front seat of the car to smile my approval on the young couple. It was the morning of their wedding day, and the four of us were on our way to pick up the marriage license at the county seat in preparation for the wedding service to be held at two o'clock that afternoon. The bride and groom were already dressed for their wedding, Yvonne in an exquisitely tailored suit and frilly blouse, Gene in a dark blue suit. It *was* going to be a beautiful wedding and a very different one than either of the young people had expected only a short while before.

Yvonne and Gene were both orphans. Because she had no one to look after her, Yvonne had been made a ward of the court. Afternoons and evenings she worked at the Longmore Café with her friend, Gloria, the Longmores' granddaughter.

When the court prepared to appoint a guardian for her, Yvonne asked that she be put in Sister Longmore's charge, and her request was granted. The Longmores took the attractive young girl into their home, where she shared in their family life.

When Delbert came into the area, he became acquainted with the vivacious young Catholic and engaged her in serious conversation concerning her faith. Night after night she gathered with the others in the Longmore living room and listened intently while Del explained the gospel of the Restoration message. It was all new to her, and the fear that she was committing a sin even by listening haunted her from her early training.

When Del approached her about baptism, Yvonne was thoroughly frightened. What if the priest was right and Delbert did preach a false religion that would damn her? The things he said sounded so right, and he did back them up with scripture; but what right had she to interpret scripture? Only the priest could do that. "Ask God!" the seventy urged. How could she ask God when the only prayers she knew were written down in a book for her, and none of them said anything about the strange things of which the seventy spoke.

"You don't have to decide right now," my husband assured her. "And don't let any one pressure you into it. We'll still love you if you remain a Catholic all your life. It's just that we believe we have so much more of the truth to offer you in the Restoration that we want to share the joys and the freedoms of Christ's way with you. Pray about it; study it out for yourself; ask any questions you want to ask; and then make up your mind."

Even after she had made the decision and had asked to be baptized, Yvonne continued to be fearful. What if it was the wrong thing to do? What if she would have to spend eternity in hell for her decision? As the moment of baptism drew near the uncertain girl was so scared she thought of running away, of backing out, of doing anything but going through with her commitment.

But something inside gently persuaded her to remain. Encouraged by the loving concern of the family and Del's assurance, "You'll never regret what you do this day, Yvonne, I promise you for your Lord," she was baptized. As the elders' hands rested on her head for the baptism of the

Holy Spirit, her fears subsided and the frightened girl was wrapped in a mantle of peace.

* * * * *

When Delbert returned to the Iron Range he found Sister Longmore very perturbed. Yvonne had met a young man of whom her guardian disapproved and was insisting on seeing him in spite of all objections.

"I just can't keep her anymore." Nellie's concern caused her voice to tremble. "I don't want to turn her back to the court, but I don't know what to do!" Tears crept down the motherly cheeks and were brushed away with a flick of the gingham apron that covered her generous figure. "I can't be responsible for her marrying him!"

The way she said "him" told Del much about her evaluation of the young man.

"Let's think about it awhile," Del suggested, "and ask the Lord for direction. After all, she is one of us now, and it would be a dreadful thing to . . ." He did not finish the sentence. "Do you suppose I could meet this young man?"

"Oh, he'll be here," Nellie spoke certainly. "He always comes in on Saturdays."

It was about nine that night when the tall, dark-haired young man came to the café and sat in a booth waiting for Yvonne to finish her work. My husband strode to the booth and introduced himself. "May I sit down and talk to you while you wait?" his question was punctuated by a friendly smile.

"Sure." Gene shrugged his shoulders and moved toward the wall.

"Have you lived around here long?" Del inquired.

"All my life." The young man responded cordially. "Of course, I haven't been around much lately. I just got back from the service."

This was common ground. Delbert had spent three years in the Navy during World War II, so they talked freely.

"What do you have in mind now?" Del liked this young man. He was forthright, poised, clean in speech and apparently in habits.

"I'm working out at the mines this summer," Gene informed him, "but I plan to go to college this fall. You see, I finished my high school while I was in the service, and now I want to take advantage of my GI assistance for an education."

"What do you want to study?" At least he was ambitious.

"I want to be a teacher," Gene announced resolutely. "I think I can make it, too, with my GI income and work I can get on the side."

* * * * *

"You know, he may not be as bad as you think," Del tried to calm Sister Longmore's fears. "He impressed me as being a very capable young man. What would you think if we took Yvonne back to the city with us?" he suggested. "I'm sure we could arrange with the Olsons for her to use the third-floor bedroom and she could eat with us. Maybe she could get a job for the summer there."

"Maybe that would be the answer," Sister Longmore agreed. "I would certainly rather do that than turn her back to the court."

"We'd love to have her," I said. The thought of turning my young friend out on her own had distressed me, and the proposed solution seemed an answer to prayer. "If Yvonne would want to come..." I added as I remembered the bleakness of the third-floor room and the plainness of our own tiny apartment we would be asking her to share. Besides, to go to the city would mean leaving the young man to whom she seemed so attached.

Yvonne agreed to the new arrangement almost eagerly. Once in the city, she had no difficulty getting a job. She was given job responsibilities at the rest home at which she was employed far beyond those of other nurses' aids with whom she worked. Years of experience in the restaurant had given her poise and confidence. Alert, intelligent, attractive, she was more mature than many eighteen-year-olds. Her employers would gladly have retained her as a steady employee, but Yvonne and Gene were making other plans.

Then one night Gene arrived in the city unexpectedly. It happened to be a night when Yvonne's employers had given her two tickets to a water carnival held annually in Glenwood Park near our home. As soon as she had received the tickets she had invited me to attend the extravaganza with her. When I learned that Gene had made the two-hundred-mile trip into the city just for the evening, I suggested that Yvonne use the ticket for him. Yvonne refused.

"I asked you," she insisted, "because I wanted you to go with me. He can just go to a movie or do something else until I'm free."

The carnival was so fascinating that I was totally immersed in the show and had completely forgotten about the waiting young man, when all of a sudden there was impressed on my mind a clear picture of Gene Tardy and my husband seated in front of a congregation of the church ministering together. With the picture came the assurance that this young man was of unusual worth and the Lord had need of him. From that moment I had no fear of Yvonne's love for Gene.

"Gene has asked me to marry him," Yvonne confided one day.

"When do you plan for the wedding to be?" I asked.

"Oh, we can't have a wedding!" Yvonne asserted. "Couldn't Delbert just marry us?"

"I'm sure he will marry you," I assured her, "but let's make it a real wedding."

"We can't afford a real wedding, Mildred. You know that." There was reproach in her voice. "I couldn't even afford a long dress."

"You don't have to have a long dress for a real wedding. We'll find one that you can wear for a long time." I bubbled with excitement. "Where do you want to be married?"

"Our friends are up on the Iron Range." Yvonne spoke hesitantly, still skeptical about the possibility of a real wedding for them.

"Where could we have it up there?" I questioned. "If we only had a church!"

"Sometimes people use the City Hall," Yvonne ventured.

"The City Hall?" I questioned, remembering the city halls I had known.

"Oh, it's beautiful!" Yvonne assured me.

Sister Longmore was not so enthusiastic when she heard of Yvonne's plans, and protested, "But she isn't through school!"

"I know that," I had raised the same question with Yvonne. "But she is eighteen; they're both alone in the world; and they both plan to go on to school. After seeing her at work this summer and after living with her these months, I have a lot of confidence in her good judgment. They're a level-headed couple of young people. And, Nellie," I continued, "I had a strange thing happen to me this summer that has materially influenced my feelings in the matter." Carefully I related my experience at the water carnival.

"I'll have to see that day!" Nellie responded. It was difficult to believe that the young man who apparently had no religious inclinations would ever sit on the rostrum of the church with Delbert.

Apprehensively Sister Longmore gave her permission for

the wedding and volunteered to make the wedding cake.

We were delightfully surprised with the Bovey City Hall. The spacious meeting room was handsomely appointed with brightly polished hardwood floors, generous windows fitted with Venetian blinds and tastefully draped. There was a sturdy but graceful podium, well designed furniture, and a baby grand piano. Off to one side of the meeting room was a kitchen just right for the preparation of the reception refreshments.

The church family joined together to give Yvonne her memorable wedding. Elsie Bennett, church organist of the Minneapolis congregation, made the trip to play. Yvonne had asked her best friend to do it, but she was a Catholic and the priest would not permit her even to attend. Rosemary Fishburn sang, and her husband recorded the proceedings on film. I prepared the reception with the assistance of church women. Sister Longmore produced an exquisite cake. Delbert conducted the service before an altar on which the Scriptures lay open on a velvet draping between two candelabra. Brother Thomas prayed God's richest blessings on the young couple and their new home. It was truly a beautiful wedding, graced by the presence of the Master of men.

GENE MAKES HIS COVENANT

Several weeks passed after Gene and Yvonne's wedding before Delbert and I returned to the Iron Range. He was to be there for a Sunday service, but we arrived a day early to have time to see the recently married couple, drawn by loving concern for the Tardys' welfare as a new family and by our desire that Gene should know the Christ who had drawn them together and had given his bride the vast family that loved her. Delbert wasted little time bringing up the subject of Yvonne's religion.

"I know Yvonne is a Mormon," Gene spoke uneasily. "I didn't want to ask any questions because I didn't want to embarrass you or her."

Del threw back his head and laughed boisterously.

"What's so funny?" Yvonne and I peered curiously from the door of the kitchen of the attractive farmhouse the newlyweds had rented.

"I just asked Gene if he had any questions about Yvonne's faith, and he says he's afraid he'll embarrass me if he asks any." My husband continued to smile broadly. "Gene, I promise. No question you can ask will embarrass me one bit. Just fire away."

"Well," the young man hesitated, still not quite certain how his comments would be received, "I know you believe in polygamy."

"You mean you knew Yvonne's church believed in polygamy and you still married her?" Del pretended to be serious.

"I was sure I could take care of that," Gene smiled and spoke confidently. "I am that much of an egotist." By now Yvonne and I had joined the men at the table, and Gene reached out to touch his wife's hand affectionately.

"Gene," Delbert was serious now, "that's one you will never need worry about. In Yvonne's church, *Christ's* church," he corrected, "one man has one wife as long as they both shall live. Don't you remember pledging to keep yourselves wholly for each other and from all others during your lives when you took your marriage vows?"

"I thought that was a strange vow," Gene admitted, "for people who believed in polygamy."

"Gene, that vow was written back in 1835, during the early days of the Restoration. It expressed Joseph Smith's view of marriage and has never been changed by Christ's church. You're thinking of another church—one led by Brigham Young after Joseph was murdered. The church Brigham Young took to Utah has a name very similar to the church to which Yvonne belongs, but it has vastly different beliefs."

"But wasn't Joseph Smith a polygamist? I've heard he had seventeen wives."

"Joseph Smith had one wife—Emma—as long as he lived," Delbert assured him. "All the rest claimed for him were given to him after he died by Brigham Young in quasi-religious ceremonies in which Joseph had no part." My husband was all minister now, intent on helping his young friend understand the truth.

"I know Brigham Young claimed that Joseph instituted the doctrine of polygamy. The idea had been advanced by some before his death. Just a month before he was killed, he and his brother, Hyrum, denounced the doctrine in no uncertain terms and expelled an elder from the church for teaching it."

"But what about the Book of Mormon?" There was still a question in Gene's mind. "I know Yvonne has one. Doesn't it teach polygamy?"

"Get me your Book of Mormon, will you please, Yvonne?" Del requested, and when he had the book he held it open for Gene to read.

"Here, Gene, read in the second chapter of Jacob what the ancient American prophet had to say about polygamy."

" 'For there shall not any man among you have save it be one wife,' " the young man read, " 'and concubines he shall have none; for I, the Lord God, delighteth in the chastity of women.' Well, that's pretty clear!"

"See here on the page before," Del pointed over his friend's shoulder. "Jacob refers to the practice of polygamy by David and Solomon as recorded in the Bible. These people in ancient America had the records we have as the Old Testament up to the time of Isaiah," he explained, remembering that this was Gene's first introduction to the new world scripture. "Speaking for the Lord he says, 'Behold, David and Solomon truly had many wives and concubines, which thing was abominable before me, saith the Lord.' He goes ahead to say that that was one reason he led the people now in America out of Jerusalem, so he might raise up righteous seed among Joseph's progeny. You remember the Joseph of the Bible who was sold into Egypt?"

"No," Gene confessed frankly, "I don't know anything about the Bible—not even the simplest stories. I've been thinking I would like to purchase a set of Bible stories for children so I could catch up a bit. Do you think that would help?"

"I think that is a marvelous idea," Del agreed.

Gene's fears were gone now. Work was forgotten, and for hours they talked of the Christ, of the Scriptures, and of Christ's church.

"It is a marvelous work and a wonder!" Delbert affirmed when the time came that he had to leave. "When I come back to stay a few weeks in the spring, would you really like to study further?"

"Yes, I would," Gene spoke fervently. "But we will be living over by the college then."

"Don't worry," Del said, "I'll find you, and we'll work on your time schedule. We won't always have to have sessions that last all day as this one has."

When Delbert returned in the spring Gene was a busy man. In addition to his full schedule of classes, he had been chosen by his school to represent the student body in welcoming visiting dignitaries, presidential hopeful Governor Adlai Stevenson and U.S. Senator Estes Kefauver, to the campus and hosting them during their stay. He was playing a lead part in the drama being produced by the college and supplementing his GI assistance income by driving a school bus. How he managed to spend time every day discussing religion was a source of constant amazement to my husband and a vibrant testimony of the young student's desire to know the Christ. At the end of Delbert's stay, Gene made his covenant with his Lord.

By now the Saints on the Iron Range were meeting in the Coleraine City Hall. This season Ernest and Nellie Longmore had spent the winter in Texas with two of their daughters, and the Saints remaining in the area had carried on without their help. On the last Sunday of Del's stay they returned to their home and went immediately to the meeting, arriving after the service had begun.

As Nellie entered the broad hall door, she stopped abruptly and almost cried out in surprise. On the rostrum directly in front of her sat Yvonne's husband with Delbert and Brother Thomas. The elders were preparing to lay their hands on Gene's bowed head for the confirmation of his water baptism by the baptism of the Holy Spirit. Quietly the Longmores took their seats and there Nellie silently wept tears of joy as God confirmed in her his pleasure at the commitment of this precious life.

* * * * *

The Tardys went on to school. Yvonne finished high school and later went to college when her children were all in classes. Gene became a teacher and with his master's degree headed his department in a large California school system for many years. He now heads the graphic arts and audiovisual department of a college there.

NEW SHOES FOR BABY GENE

"Now you won't have to wear those old shoes anymore!" I accidentally overheard Donna talking thankfully to her young son as she walked briskly down the aisle cuddling him tightly in her arms. Donna and the baby had just left the pastor's study where I knew Delbert and Brother Thomas had administered to baby Gene only moments before.

"Our Father," I prayed fervently, "please justify such faith as this mother has in thee."

The young woman was quite new in the faith, although her parents and her grandparents before them were members of the church. As a young man her father declared he had had enough of church going and with his family had lived a life of isolation from the church for years. When Del found Curtis and Ivy listed on the district records, he began to stop by the Rambo-Pederson poultry farm as often as he could make it into the area. There he shared his testimony while he picked chickens, cleaned brooders, or just visited in the comfortable old farmhouse the two families shared, eating Ivy or Donna's luscious cooking and talking with them about the good news of the kingdom and the need of the infant group in St. Paul for their participation.

Later Curtis vowed my husband had pestered them into returning to church, but I noted unmistakable pleasure in his demeanor and a twinkle in his eye each time he voiced the accusation. Especially was this true when he thrust his card case into my hands and said huskily, "Look! Your husband is responsible for that!" I looked and brushed away a tear of joy to keep it from dropping on the priesthood card enclosed.

So we had known baby Gene from the day of his birth.

"Clubfeet," the doctor diagnosed as he examined the infant. "We will start treating those feet as soon as he is able to wear shoes."

The specially-made brace shoes were put on Gene very early. Because he was growing so rapidly a new pair had to be purchased every six weeks. Each pair bore a price tag far above that which the Pedersons were really able to pay. Now at district conference Donna had brought the child to ask of the Lord that blessing of healing for which she now gave thanks.

* * * * *

"I don't understand it." The nurse was puzzled when next the Pedersons brought Gene in for his checkup and the doctor revoked the prescription for corrective shoes. "This is the first time I have known Dr. Shaffer to make a mistake!

When he puts braces on a child, that child always needs them until he is at least six!"

"Oh, Dr. Shaffer did not make a mistake," Donna was quick to reply. "Gene did have clubfeet, but the Lord has healed him!" And she explained to the startled nurse how she had taken her young son to the elders of the church and how it was in response to their prayers that braces were no longer needed.

"Oh, sure!" the nurse said scornfully. Such an event was incomprehensible to her. All she really understood was that the child who had needed treatment was suddenly without that need.

FIRE!

"You won't need to come home tomorrow." Though the words of the long distance call came through the telephone receiver distinctly, Delbert was so startled that for a moment he could think of no response except to ask Brother Olson to repeat them.

"What was that?" he questioned seriously. I held the morsel of food I was about to eat poised in the air, halfway to my mouth, and listened intently to my husband's side of the conversation.

"I said, you won't need to come home tomorrow," Brother Olson repeated carefully. "You can take a longer Christmas vacation. You have nothing to come home to."

"Nothing to come home to!" Del was obviously puzzled.

"What is the matter? What do you mean?" I dropped my food to the plate and ran to stand beside my husband at the phone.

"We've had a fire," Hans explained. "You had just as well stay there until the house is repaired and your apartment is ready."

"Fire?" Delbert repeated. "How much damage was done? Was anyone hurt?"

"No one was hurt. It happened while we and the Thomases were at work. But the house is badly damaged and..."

"And our things," Del interrupted, "are they all destroyed?" My heart stood still as I awaited the answer.

"No. Nothing of yours burned, but there was a lot of smoke damage." I breathed a long sigh of relief.

"I think we'll come on in," Delbert said. "There will probably be lots for us to do. We'll be in tomorrow night. Will there be a place we can sleep?"

"Oh, yes," Brother Olson assured him. "The downstairs was not burned. We're still living here. We'll find you a bed."

We had left our small three-room apartment for the Christmas holidays with family and friends. This was our last night out, and we were having dinner with the Ingrams in Del's hometown when the call came.

Monetarily, we knew there could be little loss. In the first place, we carried good fire insurance. In the second place, our possessions were not worth a lot of money. All that could be squeezed into the tiny makeshift apartment was there, but most of it was secondhand or makeshift. Only our wedding gifts, books, and mementos were of real value.

We entered the living room, which doubled in turn as Del's study, company bedroom, company dining room, and my sewing room, from a hall completely bare except for the black rubber treads that topped each step of the stairs. I appreciated those treads; they protected baby Alan's knees from splinters when we taught him how to negotiate the stairs as soon as he could crawl. From the west end of the hall a door opened into the bathroom which we shared with the patriarch and his family who had two rooms at the other end of the hall. Brother and Sister Thomas had become "Grandma" and "Grandpa" to young Alan.

Inside the apartment the floor was covered by an imitation oriental rug that had been beautiful once but we had purchased it for thirty dollars from someone ready to discard it. Straight ahead was the Simmons bed which just fit into the alcove made by the bay window that flooded the room with light. This did double duty as a divan and as a bed for our frequent guests. The upholstery was a shade of red that just happened to pick up a color in the rug. We bought it because it was the only good piece of furniture that could be purchased for one hundred and five dollars—a drastically reduced price because of the peculiar color which other homemakers would have had difficulty fitting into their color schemes.

Just inside the door and to the left was a desk. We had looked long and hard to find one with drawers wide enough to hold the stencils Delbert needed in his work. He had extended the desk's usefulness by placing a board atop a couple of orange crates beside it to serve as extra shelving. The desk was small but substantial and cost us thirty-two dollars new.

Along the wall that we shared with the Thomases, Del had stacked the bookshelves. Somewhere he had found some thin boards—scraps from a plywood lumber pile, I suspected—and had carefully varnished and waxed them. Bricks separated the boards into units just right for the books that needed to be available for our study and pleasure. "We can move the boards easily," he had explained, "and we'll get new bricks wherever we go." Above the books hung the only piece of real art we owned—an oil painting depicting Western Iowa, executed as a wedding gift for us by Wathena Ballantyne.

The low file cabinet at the end of the bookshelves I had pressed into service as an end table for the divan by covering it with a crocheted doily and setting our one table lamp (also a wedding gift) on it. At the other end of the Simmons we had a TV table built like a lazy susan. We did not have a television, but the table was cheap and we needed something to support the tiny radio-record player which we felt was an absolute essential for introducing our young ones to good music.

The west side of the room couldn't accommodate many furnishings. There was space for the cabinet sewing machine my family had given us and the wicker basket that was always filled with clothes to be ironed or mended. The rest was an archway where there once had been double doors. Filmy curtains dressed the bay windows without shutting out the light. And there were two straight chairs and a typing table on casters. A corner of the tabletop was missing (Delbert had bought it at a bargain).

Through the open archway one could always see the chenille-covered bed. There was no way to hide it. The imitation maple set—mattress, springs, and all—had been bought for sixty dollars from the former occupants of our first home. Since the telephone hung on the wall of the arch, I often had the ironing board set up beneath it so I could iron every time a call promised to be lengthy. There was a beautiful baby's crib—we had splurged on that—but Alan's clothing and supplies were stored in orange crates curtained by a yellow print covered with kittens and balls and other paraphernalia calculated to be appropriate for a growing boy to admire. A print of Sallman's "Head of Christ" graced the bedroom wall, and there were soft green rugs on either side of the bed to cushion bare feet from the cold wooden floors.

There were no cupboards. A pantry had been made where the door had been removed from an old closet that had once opened into a hall from one bedroom to another (the other bedroom was now the kitchen). Across the hall from the storage area the door had been boarded up and shelves installed that were barely wide enough to accommodate dishes. I had hung a cloth around them to help keep out the dust and to curtain them from view.

The tiny kitchen likewise was crowded with necessary but secondhand equipment except for a beautiful electric oven the Chandlers had given us for a wedding gift and the drop-leaf formica table. Maybe the table was a luxury. I had suffered innuendo from a clerk who had not been able to provide me with the kind I wanted. He accused me of just wanting to be stylish instead of practical when I knew that I had to have a narrow center and long leaves or there would be no place for people in the tiny kitchen, and no one could ever get through the door. As it was, dishes always had to be done quickly after a meal. Nobody could leave the kitchen until the table was cleared and the leaf dropped. If there were too many people for one leaf of the table, it had to be carried into the living room and extended there. Cheap grey folding chairs with cheerful red seats that had been purchased with saving stamps completed the kitchen accoutrements.

Several things were stored in the attic. There were a rug that the moths ate up while we weren't looking, a box of precious photographs and mementos of our youth, boxes of books (mostly from college and from my days as a member of the Book of the Month Club), a few chairs we pressed into use when the number of guests outnumbered the folding chairs and the two straight ones. Extra clothes were up there, too, for the tiny closet in the bedroom barely held enough for one season at a time. And there was some precious bedding, especially four wool comforters my mother had made us for a wedding gift from wool from the Nelson flock. All of the family had worked quilting the wool into battings, leaving drops of blood from needle pricks on some more clumsy fingers. I particularly remembered big, strong Uncle Steve—in whose rough fingers the needle just would not fit—who quickly left his sample of blood on the batting.

Although the loss could not add up to much there were those irreplaceables that really mattered—autographed books (all personal gifts of the authors), pictures, records, and mementos. . . .

I jumped from the car almost before it stopped its forward motion and ran with Alan in my arms for the side door with Delbert close behind. Through the door and up the stairs we rushed, flung open our apartment door, and stood gasping in amazement. There sat all of our living room furniture in the middle of the room covered with a plastic tarpaulin. The firemen had taken time to protect the furnishings before they sprayed water on the fire! Even the oil painting had been snatched from the burning wall and suffered only a puncture in the frame and smoke and dirt on the face of it. There was a corner of the rug burned, and the paint of the desk was blistered. That was all. The rest was smoke damage.

"How did it happen?" The question was probably not important.

"We're not sure," the Olsons responded. "It started in the third-floor bedroom where our daughter and her husband had spent the night. The firemen think he must have left a cigarette burning somewhere."

The insurance agent came promptly and proved to be a real friend. Whether the fact that he claimed the same university that Delbert and I did for our alma mater had anything to do with it, our cordial reminiscence was prelude to a generous settlement: thirty-two dollars for refinishing the desk, six dollars to clean the painting and repair its damaged frame, one dollar each for the books (that totaled more than a hundred dollars), thirty dollars for the rug, and five dollars a day for four days to hire a woman to help with the laundry. I immediately asked if I could hire myself and was assured that the insurance money would be given us and we could hire whomever we chose. The total was more than four hundred dollars—more than we had had at once since becoming a part of the missionary arm of the church—and most of it was ours to keep. The rug was turned so the burned corner did not show. Del refinished the desk—work he loved to do when there was time for it. Only the six dollars were spent for professional repair of the picture.

My husband was very tired from the long drive and the hours spent rearranging the furnishings in preparation for the repair crew. "I think I will go to bed early," he announced before supper. "I don't feel very well."

When I checked a few minutes later, I found him buried deep in the covers, his flushed face and glassy eyes giving instant witness to his raging fever. The flu had struck quickly and hard. All of my efforts to reduce his temperature were ineffective. I hated to disturb the doctor at that time of night. Then there was a knock at the door.

"We came to administer to Delbert," Bob Fishburn announced, pointing to his companion, Walter Curtis. I admitted them to the crowded little downstairs bedroom which the Olsons had graciously permitted us to occupy.

"We came at the specific direction of the Lord," Bob explained. "God told us to come to administer to you," he repeated the reason for their presence so Delbert would not misunderstand.

"If God sent you," I spoke for my husband wondering

how they even knew that he was ill, "of course you must follow his direction." Del nodded his agreement.

Seeing how ill he was, they moved quickly to the bedside, anointed him with oil, and offered their prayers. While their hands were still on his head, moisture relieved his parched tongue, his headache vanished, his fever broke, and soon the bed was wet with his perspiration.

Delbert's strength returned quickly. With the coming of the repairmen to rejuvenate the house, we accepted the gracious hospitality of Sister Tracy, and from her comfortable little home Delbert resumed his ministry.

HEALING A HOME

The gray dawn of winter still lingered over the city. A thaw had left dirty patches of honeycombed snow clinging to the northern terraces, lacing the ravines through the wooded areas and loitering in the darkened alleys. An icy chill hung over the earth, but we scarcely noticed as we threaded our way through the early morning traffic—our minds intent on our mission as we prayed for its success.

Previous plans for the day had been quashed when Dora had telephoned just minutes before. From the sound of her voice, I knew there was need for haste, although there was no hysteria... a calmness that spoke of end-of-the-rope determination that brings resolution to an impossible situation.

"I just called to tell you good-bye," Dora had said resolutely. "I am leaving this morning never to come back."

"The children... are they going with you?" I asked, concerned for the six beautiful children whose lives were being sacrificed in the melee of domestic turmoil the Arvins were experiencing.

"I have no way to support them." Dora's resignation was complete. "I am going alone."

"Can you wait a few minutes?" I knew the call was not really a simple "good-bye" but an urgent plea for Delbert to try once more.

For weeks now he had been involved with ministry to the Arvin family. He had taken me with him to visit their home when he discovered that David Arvin was listed on the church roles but was never seen at church in the city. Dora was a member of another faith, but they did not attend her church either.

Delbert was received graciously by the Arvins, and soon there were cottage meetings in progress in their home. Even the children looked forward eagerly to his weekly visits. Dora's response to the gospel he brought was one of joyful delight.

"I have a job," Dora announced one night. "I am going to work."

"Are you?" Del replied questioningly as he looked at the children ranging from twelve-year-old Marcia down to baby Charles and prayed for direction.

"Oh, we have it all worked out." Dora was eager. "I will work at night. David will be at home while I am gone. I will be here while he is away."

"That's fine." My husband was not enthusiastic, but he knew that the support of the large family weighed heavily on David alone. "Where will you work?" he asked.

"Down there." Dora pointed through the kitchen window to an all-night restaurant a few blocks from the Arvin home.

Everything seemed to be worked out perfectly, but when we came again to the home, it was apparent that all was not well. David was moody, aloof, distressed. Dora was puzzled, wide-eyed with disbelief.

"She's got a lover," David accused as he looked disdainfully at his wife. "She just went to work so she could meet him every night!"

"It is not true!" Dora protested tearfully, the utter impossibility of such a development evident in her voice and expression. "It is *not* true!" she turned weakly toward Delbert with both hands extended in a gesture of despair. "I went to work because we needed the money, but I'll quit now. I'll never go again if it bothers David."

"Wouldn't do any good to quit now," David spoke bitterly. "She'll just meet him when I'm at work!"

My husband listened for a long time, asking an occasional question until it was evident that there was need for more than simple counseling here.

"David," he finally proposed, "things are a long way from right between you and Dora. You are sure Dora is untrue to you. Dora is just as sure that you are wrong. Do you suppose a professional counselor—maybe a psychiatrist—could help you straighten things out?"

"I'm not sick!" David was recalcitrant. "She's the one who is sick!" and he pointed sternly at Dora.

"I will go gladly," Dora answered. "I will do anything to have things right in our home again!"

So it was agreed that David and Dora would see a counselor. The appointment was made with the psychiatrist and kept. When the physician suggested special tests for David, however, the irate husband put a stop to the visits.

"He thinks I'm the sick one!" he explained scornfully, irritated that anyone could not see that it was Dora who was really ill.

Delbert suggested the advisability of continuing with the doctor until they were sure they were both well. Dora was anxious to follow through, but David was adamant. Never! Never would he be subjected to tests designed to see if he was sick in the head! He had gone at first only to get Dora there so he could prove how she had been lying to him.

Del left the city for a three-week missionary journey and had no further contact with the family until Dora's call. "Oh, God," he prayed, "it must be bad out there. Please go before us and prepare the way that we can minister for thee in this home."

In a clump of evergreens near the top of a long slope that overlooked the city nestled the Arvins' home—a neat white bungalow trimmed in soft coral. Even the bleakness of winter could not rob it of its charm in the morning light. Crisp curtains framed the kitchen windows against which the glow of the lamp silhouetted the two waiting occupants.

Inside the house, David sat dejectedly at the table drumming aimlessly on the bright checked cloth with his right hand while his left clung precariously to the pocket of his jeans, held there by a loosely hooked thumb. Dora wandered about the room wiping up imaginary crumbs from the polished work surfaces, straightening towels already meticulously smoothed over the racks, reclosing drawers and repeatedly glancing toward the driveway, anxious to see the seventy's car there.

Preparations for Dora's departure were complete. Breakfast dishes were washed and put away. The house had been put in order even at this early hour. The older children had caught the bus for school. Dora's clothes were packed.

Our arrival brought a look of relief and hope to Dora's countenance. Although David was embarrassed, he too greeted us expectantly.

The day dragged by. Just when it would seem that

progress was being made, David would always retreat into a barrage of accusations and stubborn assertions that it was all Dora's fault and he would never submit to interference from anyone—doctor, counselor, anybody! Frequently he would stride to the window and point accusingly to the restaurant below which he identified as the seat of his family's troubles. About four o'clock he suddenly left the room.

"He has gone for his gun!" Dora whispered her fears hoarsely. "He has threatened to use it before. He has gone for it now." Her fear was near panic.

I looked hard at Delbert. "What will he do now?" I questioned silently. "What can he do?" And as I questioned I prayed for divine direction for my husband.

Del never moved from his seat by the table. "It's all right," he assured Dora. "You don't need to be afraid." I saw my husband's head tilt slightly forward in the hand he had braced on the kitchen table, and knew that he too was praying.

The door opened briskly as David returned to the room. His hands were empty. In four quick strides he crossed the room and again stood at the window overlooking the all-night restaurant. The three of us waited breathlessly for his next move. Slowly he turned from the window, rhythmically tapping one hand into the other. Across his face played an embarrassed smile. His eyes were moist. "Haven't I been silly?" he questioned simply and his voice shook a little with the intensity of the emotion that filled his frame.

The moments that followed are sweet in the memory of Dora and David. We stayed just long enough to help the happy couple express their thanks to the Source of their happiness and to help them design a plan for their family altar. When we left we were quietly assured by the firm handclasps and the sheer joy that illuminated both David and Dora that this turn of events was for keeps.

"What happened?" I questioned, as my husband guided the car back across the city in the afternoon traffic.

"When David left the room," he explained gratefully, "I was instructed of the Lord to pray that the evil spirit which possessed him would not return with him—that it would be removed never more to have power over him. And it was done even as I prayed!"

CO-CREATORS WITH GOD

"Dr. Hass speaking." I was surprised to hear an unusual harshness in the doctor's voice. "Where are you, anyway? I thought you were coming to the hospital. I am waiting for you!"

"I'm sorry, Doctor," I apologized. "I *am* coming in, but I have to feed the children first, and I would like to eat my own supper. I'm famished!"

"Supper!" the doctor sputtered. "Don't you know I can't give you an anesthetic if you eat?"

"Don't you know, Dr. Hass," I responded firmly, "that I don't *want* any anesthetic? My babies are all born without it."

"You really meant that?" This was the first of our babies the good doctor had delivered, but I had thought he understood.

"I really mean it!" I transposed the statement into the present.

"Well," his irritation appeared to be ameliorated, "go ahead and eat supper then. How are the pains?"

"They were regular when I called in, but they have eased off now."

About four o'clock in the afternoon it had become apparent that our third child would soon be born. I called Delbert, who was three hundred and sixty-five miles away in Canada, to tell him I would be going into the hospital.

"Do you know where Brother Elvin and Apostle Oakman are?" he inquired. "I can't leave here until they arrive. We have everything set up for the special weekend, and the first service is tonight."

"They're on their way," I informed him. "They left this morning. I don't think you could possibly make it in time, anyway, so stay there as long as you are needed."

"How will you get to the hospital?" He was concerned.

"I could walk," I teased.

"Don't you dare!" he commanded. He wasn't sure I wouldn't do it, since the hospital was only a few blocks away.

"No, Bob and Rosemary are coming to stay with the children." I laughed at his consternation. "Bob will take me. Don't worry about a thing!"

"I'll be there as soon as I can make it," he promised. "And, honey, I love you."

The Fishburns arrived at suppertime. I had to laugh a little at the wide-eyed intensity with which they both watched every move I made. They were expecting their own first child in a few days, and the whole process of preparation for birth was intensely interesting to them.

After carefully explaining to Alan, who was four, and Ron, two years his junior, that I was going to the hospital so the baby brother or sister for whom they had been waiting could be born, and that Rosemary and Bob would take care of them until Daddy came, I kissed them both and was whisked toward the door by the anxious young elder.

"Will you please call Brother Hans and have him meet us at the hospital?" My final request of Rosemary was not an afterthought. Delbert had arranged before he left for Brother Olson to assist in administering to me before the baby's birth. It was not that I felt ill or anticipated any difficulty but rather that both Del and I viewed with awe the privilege of being co-creators with God and wanted to invoke his presence in every stage of that creation.

At the time of each possible conception we had prayed that should a child be conceived it would have the very best inheritance we could give it, that it might have a strong body and alert mind and be possessed of a spirit that would help it always to love and serve its God. During each pregnancy I had been especially careful to eat foods that would provide nutrients I knew would be essential to the development of a healthy baby. All my life I had tried to prepare for childbearing by following God's instructions in the Word of Wisdom so that I could claim his promise that the children I bore would be healthy. Never, to my knowledge, had I used any drug, even in well accepted social form, that might lessen my potential as a mother.

Delbert, too, had always seen to it that I was assured of his love and concern. He never criticized if the housework lagged because of my need for extra rest during pregnancy. He just pitched in and helped. And there was never a glance that would make me feel that my protruding abdomen or awkward stance was an embarrassment to him. Together we joyously welcomed each addition to our family. Sometimes we smiled, remembering the way we had filled in the questionnaire at the time Delbert was asked to accept responsibility as a full-time appointee of the church. In answer to the question "How many children have you?" we wrote "None, but we expect to have five or six." We thought that the bishop should be warned!

After all the years of preparation, I had no intention of jeopardizing the chance of claiming God's promise of healthy children to save myself a few moments of pain. I knew that the anesthetic which would ease the discomfort could also affect the child, and I had read reports in medical journals during my graduate studies that there was a chance our little ones might not be able to take those full breaths of oxygen so essential for the alert minds for which we had prayed if I had an anesthetic. Besides, I wanted to be alert to know all that was transpiring and to be able to greet our wee ones when they emerged into the outside world.

"Darling," my husband's whisper wakened me. With one swift motion he crossed the room and took me into his arms.

"What time is it?" I asked when I could get my breath.

"Just past three," he replied, holding me at arm's length to look at me—tousled hair and all.

"You mean they let you into the hospital at this time of night?" I had not expected to see him until morning.

"They couldn't help themselves." He laughed. "I came a long way to see my wife. And," he added truthfully, "the nurses were sympathetic."

"Have you seen the baby?" I knew I wasn't the only one he had come a long way to see.

"Not yet," he said, pulling me to him in an extra meaningful embrace, the kind he always gave when his love was so great he could find no words to match it.

"He looked so comical when he was born," I laughed. "... It was as if someone had squashed his chin up and his forehead down so his whole face was telescoped into a funny red caricature of himself. But he's a perfect baby," I said thankfully, "and he certainly has healthy lungs!"

THE ERRANT DOCTOR BILL

Sunday morning services were over at the little church at Fifth and Queen streets. The last strains of the postlude had died away, and the friendly chatter of the Saints had almost ceased as I wrapped baby Steven in his blankets prior to our three-and-a-half-block walk home. I was usually one of the last to leave the church, partly because I wanted to speak to so many of the people and partly because it took a long time to get two young boys into snowsuits, mittens, boots, and scarfs and the third into bunting and blankets for the trip.

"Ahem!" I looked over my shoulder without straightening up from the couch on which I had laid the baby. "Ahem!" The pastor cleared his throat again and shifted his weight from one foot to the other in obvious embarrassment. I fastened the last pen in the blanket and straightened to face my red-faced young friend, carefully bracing my legs against the couch so the little one could not roll off. I smiled reassuringly and waited for Roger to speak. Nothing I could think of had happened that could possibly justify such discomfort on the part of one usually so well composed.

"Do you . . ." the troubled pastor just could not seem to bring himself to frame the question. "Do you . . ." he began again, "know anything about a doctor's bill that your husband has not paid?" Suddenly the words tumbled out as if he must be rid of them quickly.

"For goodness sake . . ." I exclaimed, "don't tell me you have been dunned for it, too!" Then I laughed heartily.

Relieved by my reaction, Roger went on to ask, "Tell me, what's this all about?"

For months we had been receiving a bill from a doctor whom we did not know for services we had never received. Each month, I would return the bill with a note explaining that the bill was not ours.

Finally the bills began to arrive from a collection agency that became abusive in its threats against our credit rating, position, and possessions. In exasperation I called the office to once more explain that we did not know the doctor concerned, had never received his services, and would appreciate it if the proper persons were billed. I even suggested the money might be obtained that way. "Besides," I finally affirmed when it was apparent that my explanation was not being received with credulity, "my husband is a minister of the Reorganized Church of Jesus Christ of Latter Day Saints, and the church pays our medical bills. We would have no reason to withhold payment if we owed the bill!"

"So this was what came of it!" I was amused and irritated at the same time. "That secretary must really have been alert. She must have taken down the name of the church, looked up the address in the telephone directory, and promptly billed the church for somebody's delinquent payment!"

"And you don't even know the doctor?" Roger inquired. He had to be sure of his facts to implement the procedure forming in his mind.

"We never heard of him before the bills started coming," I affirmed.

"I don't think you will hear from this agency again."

Roger was not embarrassed the next time he saw me.

"What did you do?" I was curious.

Monday morning he had taken time off from his own work to call on the secretary of the collection agency. "Where did you get the address of the Delbert Smith whose bill you sent us?" he inquired after he introduced himself as our pastor.

"From Dr. Szackern," she declared.

"Did you check to see if it was the correct address?" Roger persisted.

"Well, we checked the telephone directory." Her defenses were weakening.

"And do you know it is the Delbert Smith whom Dr. Szackern had for a patient?" He pressed the question.

"Nnno," the girl admitted reluctantly. "The doctor lost track of his patient before we got the account."

"I want you to know," Roger said, "that if any one of us is ever billed for that account again, we will sue your agency for defamation of character. Do you understand?"

It was impossible not to understand the determined young man. The billings ceased.

"Roger, I want you to know how thankful I am that you did come to talk to me about it," I said. "Just think. If you had just paid the bill and said nothing, you would have gone all of your life thinking my husband a crook!" The thought distressed me.

"I guess someday we will learn that the Lord wasn't fooling when he instructed us to go to our brothers if we suspect them of evildoing. Funny how many problems could be averted that way!" Roger said. Then in a lighter vein he teased, "When Delbert comes in, tell him I want to see him about a doctor bill, will you?"

THE LATE BAPTISMAL SERVICE

A large rectangular section of the floor had been lifted from the lower auditorium of the stately old church disclosing a well-filled baptismal font around which the waiting congregation now clustered. Only one side was free of people—the side usually occupied by the ministers who would conduct the service. I stood well back from the edge of the water with my three little ones, cautioning the older ones not to get too curious about the contents of the font and wanting to be prepared to leave hastily should the youngest produce noises that might disturb the service.

"Mildred," an anxious district president approached me, his brow furrowed with concern, "where is your husband? It's time for the service to begin, and he is nowhere to be found!"

"I don't know." I was accustomed to my husband's disregard of time when important matters justified it, but he usually made it to services on time—especially baptismal services for which he was responsible.

"He was here just moments ago, so he can't be far." I scanned the room hoping to spot Delbert just arriving or deeply involved in conversation with someone. He was not there.

Actually, the boys and I had scarcely seen him in three weeks. For all that time he had been in Wisconsin's Porcupine Valley sharing the gospel. During the week just past, he had called and asked, "Could you make arrangements with the branch president there in the city for a baptismal service

Sunday afternoon? We have eight or nine people to be baptized and there is no suitable place for the ordinance out here."

"When will you be in?" I asked. "What time do you want the service?"

"We plan to have an early service here and to caravan in from the Valley," Del was calculating as he spoke. "We'll bring our lunches to eat after we get there. Oh, we'll probably be in by one o'clock and should be ready for the baptism by two. Invite anyone there who would like to join with us to come."

The past hour had been a busy one, Del had barely had time to greet me and his sons, and certainly had shared no plans that would account for his mysterious disappearance.

Time dragged on. The congregation grew restless with waiting, and the district president grew increasingly concerned. Finally the door from the kitchen hall opened and Wes's expression changed from one of concern to one of amazement. The eyes of the congregation turned to follow his gaze, and a hushed murmur rippled through the group. Tears sprang into the eyes of several, while others mirrored the radiant smile of the seventy who stood there in his usual baptismal attire—white shirt and pants and black bow tie—holding open the door for two men, also dressed in white and smiling shyly, to enter the room. Delbert escorted the men to join the cluster of others attired for their baptism and took his place in the row of priesthood men who stood ready to minister. At his nod of readiness, Wes called the group to worship. The congregation sang joyously.

"How did it happen?" Wes inquired curiously when the baptisms were completed and the newly baptized were welcomed into the family of the Saints. "George and Jake have been in-laws of the church for so many years, we thought they would never be baptized!"

"It was the Lord's doing," my husband returned. "I had finished my series of cottage meetings with them and we sat reminiscing, when suddenly it happened."

* * * * *

"You've known a lot of missionaries, haven't you?" the seventy inquired of the older man.

"Oh, yes," Jake recalled, and he named a series of ministers who had visited the area and had been in his home. They dated back nearly half a century.

"Why," the seventy wanted to know, "have you supported your wife in the church all of these years and learned about the gospel from such competent ministers, yet you've never been baptized? Is there something to which you object?"

"Oh, no!" both men assured the seventy. Then the younger man confessed hesitantly, "I guess I just never felt good enough."

With a sudden surge of inspiration, Delbert turned to George and, leveling his finger in a gesture meant to emphasize his conviction, said, "George, your trouble is that you don't really believe there is enough power in the blood of Jesus Christ to cleanse you of your sin! Isn't that right?"

George smiled sheepishly and nodded his agreement. "I reckon that's the way it is," he admitted reluctantly.

"Don't you know that that was why Christ came—to call sinners to repentance?" Del leaned forward in his earnestness and laid his hand on George's knee. "You see, the righteous don't need a Savior. Christ came for sinners like you and me. Not one of us can come into God's presence without divine atonement. Christ said, 'All power is given me in heaven and earth!' That includes the power to forgive our sins and give us eternal life. But he's not going to force you to accept his forgiveness. You have to move out in faith to receive it in the way he designed—by repentance and baptism."

"I've done all that I can," he reported to the pastor of the Valley congregation when he returned to the elder's home for the night. "Only God can bring them to take the step!"

At the early service on Sunday morning, George approached my husband. "Are you going around the highway on your way into the city?" he asked.

"That's my plan," Delbert said.

"Could we meet you at the junction?" he inquired. "We have to go by home on the way."

"Surely," the seventy agreed. "I'll meet you at the junction."

As the caravan proceeded toward the city, Del recalled that George had said he had to go by his house on the way. "I wonder if they had to pick up their clothes for the baptism?" he mused, but said nothing to his passengers of his hopeful suspicion.

When the lunch was finished, Delbert maneuvered through the crowd to the bench along the wall on which George and Jake sat together. "Did you bring clothes for your baptism?" he asked them directly.

"Yeah," both men nodded and grinned, "but we sure weren't going to tell you!" George verbalized their secret.

"Come on," Del urged. "It's almost time for the service to start. You'll have to hurry to get dressed!"

Although the seventy was aware that opening time came and went while the two men dressed, he was not about to abandon them to enter the service area alone. Their acceptance of God's gift to them and their commitment to his purposes meant too much to allow their great moment of decision to be marred by embarrassment.

ON THE RIGHT TEAM

"If you call there, be sure to ask for Mrs. Longsdorf before you tell anyone who you are," Walter Baldwin advised Delbert when he asked about the last name on the list of Minnesota Saints to be visited that Saturday. "Her husband doesn't like Latter Day Saints very well any time, and it is getting late."

Del glanced at his watch. "Nine o'clock!" he exclaimed. "How did it get to be that time of day?" The question was sincere. He had never had an accurate sense of time, and it was especially unrealistic when he was enjoying his work. He had had a good day of Saint-hunting with Walter as guide. Walter, newly baptized and enthusiastic, would have made any day a pleasant one. His sudden reluctance at the mention of the last name made Delbert very curious.

"I still think we'll try them." My husband didn't like to quit with any families on the list uncontacted. "Besides, if it could be bad, I'd rather have you along for protection—or moral support—than to come back later alone," he teased. Then seriously he said, "I honestly feel that we ought to try."

"There's the telephone," Walter conceded, pointing to a roadside booth coming up beside them. "Go ahead and try."

"She seemed startled." Del reported the telephone call to Walter. "Now I *am* curious."

The Longsdorf home would have been difficult to find at night had it not been for Walter's intimate knowledge of the area. With his direction, however, it was only a matter of minutes from the call until the two men were being welcomed cordially into the comfortable home; even Mr. Longsdorf seemed glad to see them. Certainly none of the antipathy that Walter had anticipated was evident. Del accepted the friendly greeting as normal, but Walter was obviously puzzled. The family seemed genuinely anxious to be finished with formalities and began asking a barrage of questions. Each answer was received with attention.

"Why did you come here tonight?" Mrs. Longsdorf confronted Delbert and Walter abruptly a few minutes after midnight.

"I wanted to get acquainted with all of the Saints in this area," Del responded, a bit puzzled by her sudden departure from the type of questions with which she had been plying him for nearly three hours. "And when we thought of going home without coming here, I felt the direction of the Spirit that we should see you, even though it was late."

"I have been studying with the Jehovah's Witnesses," she explained. "They are so sure of their beliefs and I was so uncertain of mine! Today I just had to know the truth." She paused to look questioningly at Delbert as though she wondered whether he would understand how she could be so confused.

He smiled and nodded for her to continue.

"All day today I have prayed for God to send me an answer. I even asked him to send me his servant to answer my questions." There was a quiver in her voice and tears glistened in her eyes as she finished, "And you have answered them every one!"

"I'm glad," Delbert said. "It's wonderful what God does for us, isn't it? Would you like for me to make arrangements to come back and hold some cottage meetings so you and your family would not have to be so unsure about the teachings of the Christ?"

"Could you? Oh, Brother Smith, if you only could come and teach us!" The earnestness of the plea touched Delbert's already joyful heart.

Plans were made for the beginning of the meetings, good-byes were said, and Delbert and Walter headed for home. So intent were they on recalling the events of the day that they were not immediately aware that the car was beginning to malfunction. When the engine failed to respond to pressure on the accelerator and finally coughed to a halt, they were far from town.

"Hey!" Del's mind came out of the clouds with a thump. "I can't have this happen. I have to be in Deerwood for a baptismal service in the morning."

"It's morning already," Walter reminded him, "and it's Sunday morning at that. How do you suppose we'll get help out here this time of day?"

"You're a truck driver," Delbert said hopefully. "Aren't you supposed to know about motors and such?"

"Yeah, a little," Walter agreed, "but I don't have any tools."

"I carry a few," Del said. "I have a hammer and a screwdriver and a pair of pliers."

"And a flashlight?" Walter questioned.

"And a flashlight!"

"We don't really have much choice, do we?" Walter stated their plight practically. "Let's have a look."

By the flicker of the flashlight, the men poked and pulled inexpertly at the motor and its fittings. Finally they agreed that the difficulty must surely be in the carburetor somewhere, and Walter narrowed it down to the float. To that object he administered a few deft taps with the hammer and the engine started.

"Thank God!" Delbert breathed a prayer of thanksgiving. "You know, I have a man depending on me to baptize him. If

I don't get there it could make a difference in his life."

"After what God has done tonight," Walter spoke positively, "I'm sure you'll make it. You're on the right team!"

GOD'S MESSENGER, THE MECHANIC

The series of meetings Delbert had held in the Deerwood area was nearly finished and he had gone to talk to Lloyd Bordwell about the baptismal service to be held in the lake nearby on the following Sunday. Several had asked for baptism including some of Lloyd's children. That Lloyd had been reared in a church family, Delbert was well aware. That he evidenced only love and respect for Christ's church and its people, my husband knew from having repeatedly been the recipient of his hospitality. Why he had not committed his life to the Christ in baptism was a mystery.

"It isn't that I don't believe. It isn't that I don't want to be baptized. It's just that I don't think it would be right for me to be baptized," Lloyd explained when asked.

"Do you want to tell me about it?" Del sensed there was some trauma in this young farmer's life which was responsible for his reticence.

"You know I had a twin brother?" Lloyd questioned.

"Yes, your mother told me. He was named Floyd, wasn't he?"

"Yes," Lloyd reminisced. "Floyd and Lloyd. We were as close as our names." He smiled a little at the recollection, then arose and with a brief glance out the window walked over to the open door and leaned against the side of it. Delbert followed slowly, not wanting to intrude on the young man's reverie but wishing to be near to hear clearly and to see what his friend was seeing.

Before the two men lay the Bordwell farmstead. There were sturdy old buildings, some needing a bit of paint, clustered near the end of the feedlots. Beyond them lay the cultivated areas almost obscured by the trees that generously bordered the fields and cloistered the crystal lakes typical of Minnesota.

"We knew every inch of it." Lloyd indicated the scene from the doorway with a sweep of his hand. "And loved it." He added thoughtfully: "See that clump over there?"

The seventy nodded.

"That was our favorite spot. Behind those trees is an old rock quarry. It was just right for diving and swimming. We could fish the lake, but for plain fun the quarry couldn't be beat."

"Floyd was a good swimmer?" Delbert questioned cautiously.

"Great! Great!" Lloyd affirmed emphatically, then promptly seemed to change the subject.

"Floyd was a better boy than I was." Lloyd shifted his weight against the doorpost and glanced briefly at Del.

"How's that?" my husband encouraged him to go on.

"Oh, you know ... he thought more about God and the church and being good. Even read his scriptures and studied his Sunday school lessons. I never had time for such things." He paused.

Delbert waited.

"Then when Brother Okerlind came through here preaching, he stayed with us. Floyd listened to him and really wanted to be baptized. Wanted me to be baptized with him.

But I wouldn't do it. I hadn't studied as he had. Didn't think I knew enough about it. Besides, I didn't feel the way he did. I just couldn't be bothered. Guess I believed in God and Christ and being good and all that, but the church was just sort of Mom's church to me."

"There wasn't a branch of the church near here, was there?" the seventy questioned.

"No. Mom had Sunday school for us and the neighborhood kids who didn't get into town for church," Lloyd explained.

"And you weren't interested?" The question was an open-ended one.

"Oh, I was interested. I just didn't take it seriously as Floyd did. Then when he died . . ." his voice trailed off at the memory.

"Floyd was young when he died?" Delbert pressed compassionately.

"He was in the service in Alaska. Died in line of duty, the government said. We never did find out how. It had to be an accident."

"He didn't get baptized?"

"He wouldn't go ahead without me, and I wouldn't do it. Can't you see?" Lloyd turned pleading eyes to the seventy, all of the guilt feelings that had smoldered in his consciousness through the intervening years mirrored there. "I kept him from being baptized. It wouldn't be fair for me to be baptized when he can't!"

"Had it ever occurred to you," Delbert did not want to offend an already troubled man, "that you might not understand how things really are with Floyd or with you? Do you comprehend what it means that Christ died for you personally?"

"What does it mean?" Lloyd was willing to listen.

"It means simply that Christ does for us that which we

would but cannot do for ourselves when we have faith in him that moves us toward God."

"What does that have to do with Floyd and me being baptized? He's dead. It's too late for him, and I can't do it without him." Lloyd could see no hope for a resolution of his dilemma.

"Looks as if you should have studied your scriptures a bit more." The seventy smiled as he chided gently. "Do you understand how much love it took for Christ to go to the cross for us?"

"I suppose not."

"I don't fully comprehend it either," Del spoke earnestly, "but what I do know of that love leaves me no room to believe that an accident like Floyd's could ever doom him forever. Don't you remember Paul's testimony? 'For I am persuaded that neither death, nor life, nor angels, nor principalities, nor powers, nor things present, nor things to come, nor height, nor depth, nor any other creature, shall be able to separate us from the love of God, which is in Christ Jesus our Lord.' "

"But he wasn't baptized," Lloyd persisted.

"Baptism is an essential principle of the doctrine of Christ," Delbert agreed, "but faith in Christ and good living may open the way to work out the baptism. John's testimony is that all who are in their graves shall hear the voice of Christ and shall come forth: 'They that have done good, unto the resurrection of life. . . .' The Scriptures teach clearly that the just who live by faith in Jesus Christ will come forth in the first resurrection and live with Christ on the earth a thousand years and more before the judgment day. What's to prevent his being baptized then?"

"Do you think he might?" The sudden shifting of Lloyd's shoulders typified a man whose burden was being lifted.

"Why don't you read about it in the scriptures?" Delbert

suggested. "I can't tell you what has happened to Floyd or what choices he has made, but I can tell you that Christ did not quit loving him when he died. Why, Christ even promised that the gates of hell would not prevail against His church and then proved it by going there to preach to the spirits in prison—some of whom were disobedient in the days of Noah. He went to preach even to those who had to be destroyed because of their wickedness, so they could live according to his gospel in the spirit. Peter tells about it in his record. I'm sure he would not have known if Christ himself had not told him. If Christ loved those wicked people enough to follow them to hell to save them, surely he loved Floyd enough to continue to minister to his needs after death."

"Then you think it might be all right for me to be baptized?" Cautious hope was replacing dejection in Lloyd's voice.

"I am sure God *wants* you to be baptized Sunday, Lloyd. I'll tell you what I would like you to do. You pray about it until Sunday and ask the Lord to help you understand his love."

At six on Sunday morning we were on our way to Deerwood after picking up Elder Gordon Bennett to go along and assist with the confirmations of those baptized. We were not out of the city when the car began to fail. For a few blocks it would run well, then it would sputter and slow down almost to a stop. No amount of pumping the accelerator or pulling the choke helped.

"This is the way it acted last night," Del said. "Walter was able to get it going again after a few tries. Maybe I can."

"Well, we'll never get there this way," I agreed. "Do you know what he did?"

"He just tapped around on the carburetor somehow, and it worked."

"I hope you know where to tap," I said skeptically.

He tapped, and the car ran a few more blocks. When it began to fail again I looked at my watch. I knew that if we didn't get going soon, there would be no hope of arriving at the lake in time for the scheduled service. "Lord, we are on your errand. Please help us," I prayed.

As the car lurched ahead momentarily I looked at my husband. I knew that he too was remembering the importance of this journey and was discussing it earnestly with his Father in heaven.

The car was barely moving as we rounded the corner that put us on the main highway, but Delbert would not give up trying. As we entered the junction, we spotted a filling station just ahead. Coaxing and praying, Del managed to maneuver the car to a chugging halt in the driveway.

"Got trouble?" The affable attendant's question was redundant.

"We certainly have," Delbert returned. "Is there a mechanic here?"

"Not on Sunday morning," the attendant answered.

"Do you know anything about carburetors?"

"Not a thing." The attendant whistled merrily as he turned his attention to opening the station.

Del tapped and tapped . . . but without response. There was no magic in his touch.

"Will we have to call and tell them that we cannot make it?" I was reluctant to admit defeat, but the time was past when we could complete the trip safely.

"Just call and say we'll be a little late," my husband instructed. "I'm sure God wants Lloyd baptized today. He won't leave us stranded here long."

I had just started inside to telephone when a man drove into the station, parked his foreign-made automobile, and walked directly to our car as though he had been called to fix it.

"Looks as if you have some trouble," he observed.

"We certainly have," Delbert responded, "This . . ." and he started to explain his problem.

The stranger interrupted him. "Do you have a float gauge?" he inquired of the filling station attendant.

"Nope," came the monosyllabic reply.

"Then how about a fine gauged ruler?" Obviously this man was no novice mechanic.

"Think so." The filling station attendant produced a small ruler from the office.

"Just a minute," the stranger said as he took a set of tools from his own car. In minutes our car was operating perfectly.

Delbert was effusive in his thanks. "What do I owe you?" he inquired expectantly.

"Not a thing!" The benefactor was firm in his refusal of compensation. "Just glad I could help." And before Delbert could return the ruler to the office, the man had sped away.

* * * * *

It was a beautiful baptismal service graced by the Spirit of God. A preaching service, potluck dinner, and confirmation service followed, after which we returned to the city. As we neared the junction at which we were to leave the main highway, we recalled the events of the day.

"Let's stop in at the filling station and find out who it was that fixed our car this morning," I suggested.

"We didn't get him properly thanked, did we?" my husband agreed.

At the station Del inquired. "We were here this morning and a man fixed our car for us. Could you tell us who he was? We'd like to thank him."

"Never saw him before," said the cheerful attendant. "He never even stayed to buy gas."

We made the rest of the trip in reverent contemplation. "God did want Lloyd baptized," my husband affirmed.

"Enough to send his messenger to fix our balky car!" I added gratefully.

NEW LIFE FOR MARIAN

When Sister Swanstrom asked Delbert to go quite a distance out of the way en route home from reunion to administer to Marian, we knew she must be more ill than usual. Neither of us, however, was prepared for the sight of the emaciated figure propped up in the hospital bed. During the months since I had seen her, flesh had seemed to melt away from her frame leaving taut skin over a skeleton grotesquely malformed by pockets of fluid that had collected in swollen joints. Her sickly yellow color testified of the liver disease that now ravaged her body. Her chest heaved with every breath, and it was evident that the elevation of her bed was a necessity for her to breathe at all.

Her words came haltingly. "When I . . . am well . . . I want to be . . . baptized."

I caught the carefully enunciated words as I opened the door of the hospital room at which I had been stationed to prevent anyone interrupting the administration. Now that the prayer was finished, I lingered in the hall since only two visitors were allowed, and the sick woman's mother-in-law and Del were at her bed.

Marian Bordwell was chronically ill with a severe heart

ailment. When her last child was born, the birth had almost taken her life. Since then, she had been restricted to minimal activity, largely confined to bed or a rocking chair set by the bay window of the old-fashioned living room from which she could sometimes catch a glimpse of Lloyd or the boys as they went about the business of farming.

Because she had never been really well, Marian depended on Lloyd and the boys to keep the household running smoothly, too. Under her competent supervision, the house was spotlessly clean and in order, and there was always homemade bread. Elmer and Gene, the older sons, saw to that. Regularly they baked the big, fragrant loaves that were a delight to family and friends alike.

"When I ... am well." The words echoed in my mind. The doctor said there was little chance that day would come. In fact, he gave no hope at all that it would ever be.

First there had been a severe attack of pneumonia complicating the heart ailment. Because the disease was so debilitating it completely sapped her meager strength. She could not orally expel the fluid that collected on her lungs so it had to be drained away by surgical processes. With the pneumonia still unconquered, hepatitis was now taking its toll.

But Marian had expressed no doubt. She did not say, "If I get well," but "When I get well."

"Oh, God," I prayed silently, "please justify her faith, performing the miracle of healing that can come only from thee."

The administration was performed late in June. Early in August word came through the nonresident pastor, Brother Thomas. "I have a letter from Marian," he said. "She wants to be baptized." "I am well now," the letter read, "and I would like to be baptized as soon as the service can be arranged."

Joyfully Delbert and Brother Thomas planned for the service to be held at Deerwood Lake where Lloyd and the boys had been baptized. The confirmation would be in Grandmother Swanstrom's home in town. Brother Thomas would give the sermonette; Del would baptize; together they would confirm.

The morning of the baptismal service a strong west wind blew over the lake, whipping the waves into billows. Marian seemed not to notice but stood radiant beside her husband as she awaited the signal to enter the water. I could not help looking at her with some anxiety.

The fragility of the woman dressed in a white dress was visible when the wind whipped open the coat her husband had thrown about her shoulders. Even August can be cool in Minnesota lake country. Delbert often teased the people about their one day of summer every year, and this was not that day.

The wind pushed steadily at her wasted frame, forcing her to cling tightly to Lloyd's strong arm. Tears welled up in my eyes when I saw the man's big rough hand close briefly in a caress over his wife's thin one. It would not be hard to guess the thankful prayer he was offering at that moment.

The pneumonia was conquered and the drainage puncture healed. Only the sallowness of her complexion gave hint of the hepatitis Marian had suffered, but she still had the chronic heart ailment. And she was so thin! My faith wavered momentarily. What if she would not be able to stand the shock of the cold water? I hardly heard the opening words of the minister for the beating of my own racing heart. Again I offered a silent prayer: "Please give her strength for this sacrament toward which she has looked so long."

I watched from the rear of the group of Saints gathered at the water's edge. The baby was asleep in the car, and I did not dare move far away.

"Here at the water's edge . . ." The wind bore the words of the hymn to me as the congregation sang, but Delbert's prayer and Brother Thomas' talk were muffled by the pounding of the waves as they broke upon the shore. Finally the time came for my husband to take Marian's hand and lead her into the water. When he beckoned she eagerly moved forward with Lloyd close beside her. For a brief moment she smiled triumphantly up at her husband as she slipped from her coat. When she reached out for Delbert's hand she gave her husband's arm a reassuring pat.

Gently she was led into the turbulent lake. When the big waves came, I could see Del pause to help her stand. Once she stumbled, and my heart stood still until she was securely back on her feet. It was apparent that she smiled her thanks.

When they reached a depth of water sufficient for the baptism, they turned to face the waiting congregation. There was a moment of preparation. Then Delbert raised his right hand and lifted his eyes to heaven. The words of the baptismal prayer were not audible on shore, but it didn't matter. Every person there could repeat them with the movement of his lips: "Marian, having been commissioned of Jesus Christ, I baptize you in the name of the Father, and of the Son, and of the Holy Ghost. Amen."

Marian's thin face was radiantly beautiful as she returned to the shore where Lloyd embraced her and wrapped her in a blanket. Del smiled happily, and the Saints returned his smile through thankful tears.

"There's an old, old path made strangely sweet by the touch divine of His blessed feet . . ." they all sang reverently.

Winter came and went. Spring's business had given way to summer's leisurely waiting for the harvest on Minnesota farms when Delbert again returned to the Deerwood area to minister.

"The folks?" Gene responded to his inquiry when only

the children appeared at the first service. "Oh, they won't be back for another month. They're in Oregon on a trip. It's sort of a honeymoon. They've been at home so close all these years. Mother has never been able to travel before, you know." The young man seemed very pleased for one left with the responsibility of the home and chores for six weeks. "They're even going to take in the World's Fair before they come back," he explained happily.

"That's great!" Delbert said enthusiastically as a sudden warm glow spread through his body. Filled with gratitude he announced the first hymn and sang lustily, "O God, our help in ages past, our hope for years to come, our shelter from the stormy blast, and our eternal home."

TREASURED MEMORY

It was midwinter in Minnesota. Two feet of new snow being whipped into drifts by a brisk north wind drove the twenty-five degrees below zero chill deep into even the most comfortably dressed of those who ventured out of doors. Delbert settled down for an evening at his typewriter as I prepared our three children for bed. The youngest was still a baby, and the oldest had just passed his fourth birthday.

"Daddy, can you pray with us tonight?" our four-year-old asked. It was a rare experience for my missionary husband to be at home with the children for bedtime prayers.

"Of course I can, son!" he answered. As he spoke he pushed the typewriter table away and arose to join us in the bedroom.

The children had scarcely begun their prayers when the telephone rang, and Del left quietly to answer it. When he returned, the prayers were finished and the children tucked snugly under their warm covers.

"That was Hollis," he announced. "He wants me to come to St. Paul. Joyce is very ill. Would you like to pray a special prayer with me that God will help Joyce get well?" he asked the little ones.

The boys, except for the baby who did not understand, crawled eagerly from their warm beds and knelt again. Each one prayed that God would help Joyce get well.

In moments Delbert was bundled up against the wintry blasts and on his way to St. Paul. I resumed my yet unfinished day's work, much of which had been postponed because of the needs of my family and others. As I worked, I prayed earnestly for Joyce's welfare and for the effective ministry of my husband.

Hours later, when the work was nearly done, concern began to creep into my prayers. Finally, there came the anxiously awaited crunch of familiar footsteps in the snow. I fairly flew to welcome Del home and learn of Joyce's condition.

When I opened the door, I scarcely noticed the biting wind or the swirling snow that swept past me into the hall. There stood my husband, braced against the wind and snow, dressed only in his suit. In his hands he held his overcoat wrapped into a bundle. He seemed to be trying to protect the coat by hovering over it, with the upper part of his body leaned far forward and twisted against the wind.

"Why are you carrying your coat on a night like this?" I gasped incredulously. "You must be frozen!"

He did not answer. Very carefully and very gently, as though he was handling priceless china, he placed his overcoat in my arms. Then he pulled back the lapel and uncovered his precious burden. There, nestled in the warmth of the overcoat, lay a very tiny baby.

"Joyce!" I gasped, "Is she . . .?"

"Joyce is very ill," he answered. "We had to take her to the hospital. Hollis is with her there, so I brought the baby."

"Where is Peter's food?" I asked looking around as if I half expected to find it deposited in a chair or on the divan.

"Peter is a breast-fed baby," he answered. "Joyce is his source of food."

"Then how . . .?" my voice trailed off with the unfinished question. If only my own baby had not yet been weaned! And Peter was so tiny—far too young to be introduced to solid foods. How would we get through the night? There wasn't even a bottle in the house!

I recovered from my perplexity and said, "Get out the bassinet." Together we fixed Peter's bed in the bassinet that had cradled our own three sons, placed it beside our bed, and retired with a prayer that Peter would make it through the night.

He slept.

Early the next morning I threaded my way through the traffic toward the hospital in St. Paul. In a little bag I carried bottles which I had purchased at the drugstore and sterilized.

"I came for milk for Peter," I told the startled nurse at the nurse's station as I extended the bag of bottles toward her. . . . Without waiting to be asked I explained who Peter was and why I had come there for milk for him.

"But Mrs. Olsen is too ill," said the nurse.

"But Peter must be fed!" I pleaded. "Won't you please ask the doctor if he can have his mother's milk?"

So it was that twice a day I made my way to the hospital to get Peter's food. Soon the crisis passed and Joyce was well again. She still had Peter by her side and was still his source of food.

But the sight of my minister husband in the snow with his coat in his arms nestling a baby never passed from my treasured memories.

WITNESSING TO A "WITNESS"

I glanced quickly about the mission house living room to see that it was in order. The knock at the door could herald a salesman, a garbage man, or any number of guests. Whoever it might be, I did not want the house to detract from the witness my family had to bear of the Christ.

I smiled at the thought that it might be the garbage man. Ever since we had arrived in the Islands we had had trouble keeping one. Garbage in this Hawaiian city was picked up by pig farmers who cooked it and used it as food for their animals. One by one the farmers with whom we had arranged for garbage removal had appeared at the mission house door to inform me that they would come no more. "Pigs no like!" One farmer had finally explained that the peelings and pits which comprised almost the entire contents of our garbage pail were not worth picking up even for the pigs. We had decided that if the current farmer quit we would just bury all that we discarded beneath the banana plants and hope it would make good fertilizer.

As my gaze swept the sunny southeast room, I noted the brightness of the *lauhala* mat that covered the floor. Even though Del could not get entirely accustomed to removing his shoes when he entered the house, and the children's bare feet were not always clean, it seemed not to be suffering from the usage it was receiving. The sturdy Filipino mahogany furniture with its bright, inviting cushions bespoke the hospitality we hoped to extend to all who came to our door. I made a mental note that I must soon get drapes for the big picture windows that filled the expanse of both the east and south walls. While the venetian blinds were attractive and gave adequate privacy, just yesterday Alan had commented on how much he liked to visit Larry's home because he felt "cozy" there. I wanted him and his friends to have that feeling in the mission house, too.

Assured that the room was clean and inviting, even though not quite "cozy," I opened the door to my caller.

At the top of the long outside stair stood a young *Haole* holding out a copy of *Awake* magazine. I immediately recognized it as the publication of the Jehovah's Witnesses. "I would like to leave a copy of our magazine with you . . ." the young man began.

"No, thank you," I replied politely but firmly.

"You will find an article . . ." the young man started to explain.

I shook my head negatively. "No, thank you!"

"Do you have some reason for not reading our magazine?" the Witness questioned as he dropped the piece back into his bag.

"Yes, I do." I was quick to accept the opportunity to inform the young man. "Your magazine does not tell the truth."

"That is what your husband told the sisters," he replied.

"Oh?" I had not known we had been visited by the Witnesses. The women must have stopped at the office door at the foot of the stairs.

"Can you tell me what was said that was not true?" The man was concerned.

"I surely can," I told him. "There was an article not long ago about the Book of Mormon and about the church Christ restored using Joseph Smith as His prophet. There were so many lies and distortions in it that it was pitiful. If you cannot do better than that on a subject with which we are thoroughly familiar, we certainly cannot trust you on subjects we know less about."

"Oh, I am sure the article told the truth." The young man was confident. "You must be the one who is misinformed. You are a Mormon, are you not?"

"No," I replied. "I am a member of the Reorganized Church of Jesus Christ of Latter Day Saints."

"Oh, yes!" He brightened perceptibly. "I used to go to that church when I was a little boy. I used to visit an uncle in Minnesota who was an elder in that church. By the way, I see you are from Minnesota. I saw your license plates on the car under the house," he hastened to explain.

"And who is your uncle?" I was sure that we knew every elder in the state of Minnesota.

"James Stauty."

"Of course I know James Stauty. He has been very kind to my husband," I said warmly. "And you are . . .?"

"I am Earl Palusky," he introduced himself. "I am the chief minister of the Witnesses here, and when your husband refused our materials from the women I decided to come and see him for myself."

"Well, Earl Palusky! What on earth are you doing outside the Church of Jesus Christ? Come on in!" I held open the door and said, "I will call Del!"

My husband came up from the office immediately and they discussed the article on the Book of Mormon and the Mormons. Earl was positive that the offending article told the truth. "I know," he insisted, "for I know all about the Mormons."

"But you do not know," Del corrected him, "or you would know that it does not tell the truth. Here, let me show you."

There followed many earnest discussions about the beliefs of both the ministers. "I want to buy the book you use to train your ministers," Del requested one day, "—not the one you sell to others... the one you use to train ministers!" He wanted to be sure there would be no mistaking which book he wanted. Earl obtained it for him, and Del went through it comparing its teachings with the scriptures and pointing out discrepancy after discrepancy to his new friend.

"Do you ever sit down with your Bible," Del asked one day, "and just ask God to help you understand it without using the materials written by the Watch Tower Society to interpret it?"

"Oh, no!" Earl was shocked at the thought. "I would not dare!"

"Why would you not dare?" Del was amazed at his fears.

"That would leave me open to be misled by the devil," he said seriously. "I could not do it!"

One day there was a short item in the newspaper announcing Earl's transfer to another island. "Shall we invite him to have dinner with us on Sunday?" I suggested. "I would like to have one more try at convincing him of the truth!"

"Let's," Del agreed, "but he is really afraid. Unless he can put aside his fears and ask God for direction, I don't think he will ever understand the truth."

Dinner around our table was accompanied by animated conversation that continued far into the afternoon.

"I see now that you are not the same as the Mormons," Earl admitted at one juncture in the discussion. "But I cannot blame the authors of that article for not knowing. If I had written it myself I would have written it as they did."

"That is just it, Earl," Del pressed his point. "That is what I have been telling you. Those who do not know the truth cannot write the truth. That is why this book, too . . ." and he held up the minister's own guide, "is filled with error. Why don't you ask God?" he pled.

"I cannot!" Earl repeated. "I cannot leave myself open for Satan to deceive me!"

When it was necessary that each of the men leave for their evening appointments, Del led the way to the car, and I descended the stairs to say "good-bye."

"I am sorry!" Earl voiced his disappointment. "I had hoped to make you Jehovah's Witnesses!"

"Earl," Del testified compassionately, "we *are* His witnesses!"

WATER CARRIER OR SON OF GOD

After Earl Palusky had gone from the Island, the next Jehovah's Witnesses to appear at our door stopped at the office downstairs. They were two very inexperienced young boys.

"Here," Del offered. "I have something for you." And he held out a tract describing Christ's church. "Do you believe in Jesus Christ?" he asked.

"Oh, yes!" the spokesman for the two returned, backing away from the tract. "We are doing exactly what he said to do . . . going from door to door preaching the gospel."

"You know, do you not, that Christ placed in his church

apostles, prophets, seventies, elders, and other priesthood to minister for him? Do you have apostles?"

"N-o-o-o," the boy stammered. "Are you a minister or something?"

"Yes, I am," Del assured them, "and I would really like to tell you about Christ and his church."

"I-I-I think you had better talk to somebody else." Both of the boys were retreating toward the door now. "We will send someone else," they promised as they walked hurriedly down the drive to the street.

Charles came one rainy fall day, shortly after the visit of the boys, with a beautiful young woman from Maui as his companion. Charles Ha'O had taken Earl's place as chief minister for the Witnesses on the Big Island, and he was certain he could succeed where his predecessor and the boys had failed.

That first day he came primed for the Mormons. With each accusation the young minister would bring against our belief, Del would simply disclaim the belief. "You see, we are not Mormons and have never believed those false doctrines," he tried to explain, but Charles drove ahead relentlessly, certain that Del was lying. Finally he gave what he was sure was a quotation from the Book of Mormon and gave the reference.

They turned to the reference. There was nothing remotely resembling the supposed quotation there.

"I must have the wrong place." Charles was flustered. "But I know it is there somewhere."

So Del turned again and again to other passages that might have been confused with the quotation Charles had given. Nothing fit.

"Oh, I know why we can't find it!" I brightened as I finally realized the problem. "You gave the reference from the Utah Mormon edition of the Book of Mormon. We are looking at the original church's book. The references would be very different."

"Really?" Charles and his companion spoke simultaneously. "You mean there really are two churches?" Charles had not believed a word Del had said until then. Now he was convinced that here at least his anti-Mormon approach was not valid.

"Let me show you," Del suggested, "what we really do believe about God's relationship to man and man's worth in God's view."

It took only minutes for him to set up his equipment, begin showing slides, and teaching the principles of the gospel of Christ. Charles and his companion listened intently, fascinated by the new story they heard.

"Well, I have really learned a lot this afternoon!" the young woman exclaimed when Del switched on the lights again. "I wish we did not have to go. I would like to hear more!" Then she remembered Charles and looked quickly at him to see how he was responding.

He was contemplating all that he had seen and heard. "I would like to know more," he said honestly.

"Okay!" Del was more than happy for the opportunity to share further. "When can you come back?"

The date was set. Charles returned with a new partner and listened intently to Del's presentation. His partner was uncomfortable and restless when he found that he was expected to listen rather than to instruct.

"Just wait outside." Charles had finally directed him. "I want to ask some more questions."

Every time Charles returned it was with a different partner, each of whom was distressed with his chief minister's willingness to learn from the seventy. Finally he was to come for a final thirty minutes to be carved from his lunch hour.

"I can stay only half an hour," he warned Del when he

made his appointment, "and this has to be my last meeting with you. They say I have been spending too much time at your house."

We were very anxious that the young minister whom we had learned to love dearly would respond in full commitment to the gospel of Christ. In fact, we fasted and prayed all day for our last opportunity to share with him.

The half hour went quickly, and Charles's companion announced that they had an appointment.

"It will have to wait!" Charles replied firmly, and he continued the conversation.

"The others are here to pick us up," his companion informed him in a few minutes.

"Tell them to wait," Charles instructed the man.

"Oh, just let them go on. We will take you where you want to go when we are through," I volunteered.

"They can wait!" Charles looked the command to his companion who left hurriedly to carry the message.

"Charles," Del inquired as he had asked Earl, "do you ever sit down with your Bible and ask God to help you understand its message without depending on any of the Watch Tower Society materials to tell you what you are to believe that it says?"

"Oh, no!" Charles was as shocked as Earl had been at the suggestion. "That would be denying the testimony of the willing and obedient servants who write the materials," he vowed. "That would leave me open to be deceived by Satan!"

"That is what Earl said!" I was surprised to hear almost the identical words coming from Charles as had been spoken by his predecessor, but I should never have said it. Charles seemed to take the similarity of response as affirmation that he was doing the right thing by not praying for direction. If Earl could not pray, neither should he!

"Charles, that is like the Catholic church," Del chided him gently. "You are just substituting the infallibility of a group of 'willing and obedient servants' for the infallibility of the Pope."

"Do not say that!" Charles spoke harshly. "I just came out of the Catholic church." He paused a long moment, thinking. "But maybe I did not come far enough!" he said uncertainly.

By now the afternoon was half gone. Every few minutes one of the group of ministers who waited in the car in front of the mission house would come to the door, knock, and signal furiously for Charles to come.

"Tell them to go on." I suggested again. "We will be glad to take you wherever you want to go."

"They can wait!" Charles was determined. "They have to wait as long as I tell them to," he declared, and I thought I understood more of the structure of the Jehovah's Witness movement than I had hitherto suspected.

"Charles, are you a Jonadad?" I asked once during the afternoon.

"Yes-s-s." Charles was startled by the question. "How did you know?"

"I have been reading in the book we got from Earl about the various classes of people you have in the kingdom you think God is building. It seemed that other more favored classes have been filled and those who come into the kingdom at this late date must be servants and water carriers for those who have been fortunate enough to go before. Do you know you could be a Son of God?" I yearned for this young friend to believe the truth.

"Oh, no!" Even the suggestion seemed to frighten him as though he would be chastised for allowing the thought to pass through his mind. "I could never be a Son of God!" he said positively.

"Then you are not led by the Spirit of God." Del took up the conversation to inform him earnestly.

"What do you mean?" Charles was puzzled.

As Del spoke he turned to the testimony of Paul written in the letter to the Romans, chapter eight, verse fourteen. " 'For as many as are led by the Spirit of God, they are the Sons of God,' " he read. "John puts it another way," he said, then quoted from John 1:12: " 'But as many as received him, to them gave he power to become the sons of God; only to them who believe on his name.' "

"If you want to follow Christ's way," Del assured the perplexed young minister, "you have to trust him. He is willing to reveal himself to you if you will just give him a chance. And if you give him that chance, he will give you power to become God's son, not just a water carrier for those who are. Christ never spoke of classes of citizens of the kingdom of God! He said we would be joint heirs with him in his Father's house."

"But I cannot." He shook his head sadly and the struggle inside him was heartbreaking to witness. "Earl could not and I cannot open myself up to be deceived by the devil!"

It was five thirty when the young minister walked slowly down the asphalt drive bordered with neatly trimmed California grass to join his waiting companions. The fragrance of gardenia blossoms drifted toward the house on the evening breeze wafting in from the ocean below. We stood arm-in-arm at the office door watching his heavy step as he turned hesitantly away from his hope and entered the car silently. Tears gathered in our eyes as our love welled up into our throats and stuck there while we longed to call after him and draw him close to his Lord. "Oh, God," the prayer was not voiced aloud, but rose simultaneously from both hearts, "continue to reach out to him. Grant that someday he can believe and trust thee and truly become thy son!"

Del met Charles casually in the library from time to time, and I saw him pass the mission house as he carried out his duties as chief minister of his sect, but never again did we have opportunity to talk to him about the hopes and desires of our hearts.

CONRAD GOES HIS OWN WAY

"I will be back at four o'clock. If you have not apologized to her for interfering with our lives by then, I will mop up this driveway with you. I will beat you to a pulp! Do you hear? Four o'clock!"

The handsome, tall, slightly graying man raged out at the young man standing near the door of the mission house. Delbert, white-faced, walked slowly toward the departing car. "Better make it five o'clock," he said. "I have a cottage meeting at four." There was not a tremor in his voice though his lips stretched unnaturally tight.

The days that had preceded the encounter had been trying ones for my husband. For many months it had been evident that Conrad, a prominent businessman and a member of the church, needed ministry. Delbert had loved this man from the first time he had met him but perceived immediately that Conrad's way of life was foreign to his profession of faith. Time after time Del had made overtures of friendliness and offered ministry. And time after time Conrad responded.

There was the Thanksgiving service when Conrad entered quite late. With long strides he crossed the church to his wife's side. She nearly burst with happiness! Then when he stood in meekness and humility and confessed his tendency to wander, his need of his Lord, and his determination to do all within his power to assist his Lord, those in the congregation took him to their hearts in forgiveness and love.

There was the Christmas season following when he worked so closely with the ministry to provide food and gifts for many of the poor of the area. Especially there was the moment when he stood linked arm-in-arm with the youth of the church, the pastors, and the rest of those who were to distribute the gifts. As the sentence prayers moved around the circle, he was touched with love and understanding that made him cry out in gratitude for the privilege of serving in the work of Christ's church. His body trembled, and tears ran unchecked down his handsome cheeks as he poured out his soul in words of love and commitment.

There was the disappointment of Christmas Day when he said he had "something to do" that would not permit him to spend the evening with his wife in our home at Christmas dinner and the great joy that followed when he decided the "something" could wait.

But no one was fooled—least of all his wife. The "something" was still there waiting, but we prayed fervently that he would be strong enough to overcome it. It had been that Christmas night, after we shared dinner and an evening of lively conversation about things that mattered, that he had said, "Now I know that this is the church of Jesus Christ and that I want to spend my life for him in it." And he added, "I never knew before that a man could love others more deeply than himself or his own family!"

Del was encouraged, but he knew the battle was not yet won.

There followed a year of nearly continuous absence from church and church activities. Conrad was friendly, and if there was money to be raised, he was glad to exert his influence. But he carefully shunted all attempts at ministry, and Del was concerned.

There was a glimmer of hope when he came again to the Thanksgiving service. But this time when he arose to voice his commitment, his words bore no evidence of repentance or contrition, and a trace of arrogance replaced the humility of the year before.

Then there had been the night when, quite late, the pastor and Delbert were called to the hospital and by accident discovered that the "something" in Conrad's life was no longer waiting. She was very real and very attractive and had a very strong influence on his life.

Although it was very late the two ministers drove to Conrad's home, for they knew his wife knew and would be waiting. There the three of them tried to think of a way that he could be reached and helped.

We visited Conrad's "something" the next day and talked to her about her association with Conrad, her future, and the problems her association with him were causing. Perhaps it was not the wisest approach to the problem, but it seemed a way—and we went with a deep love for both of them. But when she called Conrad to tell him of the visit, she did not tell him of the love that motivated the act, for she could not yet understand that kind of love.

And so today when he stormed into the drive, he was angry, very angry, that anyone—especially anyone in the church—should so interfere in his private life. For nearly an hour he had berated Delbert, venting his wrath as guilty men do by false accusations, insults, and innuendos. Del's refusal to respond in anger only served to frustrate him, and he threatened physical violence. Finding that likewise ineffective, he tried one last desperate measure.

"Do you know," his voice was more quiet now and his

eyes searched Del's face for a trace of evidence that he had hit his mark, "that I have twenty-three thousand dollars promised for a new building here that the church will never see if you do not forget about this whole affair? In fact, I have an eight thousand dollar check for the church in my desk this minute that the bishop will never lay hands on if you do not leave my private life alone!" Not a flicker of interest crossed Del's face. He had only pity for one who understood so little of life's real values.

"I am sorry," he said, shaking his head.

Conrad's voice raised in anger. "We have learned how to *really* serve Jesus Christ!" he fairly shouted. "We can get people to really give for the church! We know how to get people to give so we can feed the poor! And you," he spat the words out contemptuously, "you could not raise money to buy a lawn mower!"

Almost wearily Del replied, "It is not my business to raise money for lawn mowers." Then he turned and joined me at the foot of the long stairs that led to our living quarters above the office. Conrad's car roared away.

"What are you going to do?" I asked.

"Do?" Del spoke questioningly—as though he had been startled from a reverie. "I am going to call Charles and tell him to meet me at the church for our cottage meeting this afternoon. I don't want to be interrupted. We might be bothered here at the office."

Promptly at four the telephone rang. It was Conrad asking for Del.

"I am sorry," I told him. "He is having a cottage meeting, but he will be back at five." There was a long tirade, again interspersed with "you tell him" this and "you tell him" that.

"I think it would be better, " I replied, "if you would come at five and tell him yourself."

The voice changed to a friendly, confidential tone. "Did you know that your husband..." and there followed insinuations of unfaithfulness and misconduct on Del's part.

My heart beat rapidly, and my hands shook a little at the injustice of the accusations and the insidious way in which they were presented, but I managed to answer quite firmly, "If this is true, then you have a responsibility to bring charges against him in the church and have him removed from his position of ministry."

At five o'clock Delbert returned. Conrad never came.

Two days later a letter came from a local lawyer enclosing a statement of Conrad's withdrawal from the church. Del's heart was broken, and he wept.

AGIPITO COULD NEVER FORGET

Early Wednesday Agipito climbed the long ladder that led to his cage high in the ironworks, sprang nimbly into his seat, and skillfully checked the levers and switches that controlled the huge cranes which he operated from his vantage point. Like long, powerful fingers the great teeth lifted the heavy slabs of iron and steel into place for the workmen below and hefted the finished machinery, poles, steel plates, and what-have-you from the worktables when the workmen were through. It was hot in the cage. Fumes from the fires below made Agipito's nose twitch, and he wished he could get more fresh air. But the job was a good one—one that not just anyone could do.

The work was exacting. Only one who was alert and intelligent and skillful could manage the brawny cranes. Not only the safe transit of steel and poles and tanks and girders lay in his hands but the lives of the men who labored below him as well. One slight miscalculation of the hooks and an object weighing tons might slip from his grasp as it moved across the work area or a slight imbalance of some huge piece might cause it to swing out of its course, crushing machinery, building, and workmen in its errant path.

There were, however, moments when Agipito could sit quietly in his cage awaiting a signal to indicate the need for his services, and this was one of those moments. Suddenly it seemed to him that he was not alone. In front of him he seemed to see Delbert's face. (Del had been one of the two seventies who had first told him of the gospel of Jesus Christ.)

"Agipito," he was startled to hear Del's query, "Agipito, have you forgotten?"

Vigorously Agipito shook his head. "No." He spoke the word firmly. "No, I have not forgotten!" And he began once again to remember.

It was World War II. Agipito was a prisoner of war in his native Philippines. His Japanese guards were arrogant and cruel. The prisoners were hungry, thirsty, sick. One guard was especially difficult. Often during the long, hot days the men would beg for water. The guard would offer a cupful. Just as it reached a thirsty man's fingertips, he would spill it leaving the man grasping an empty cup. Then he would laugh a long, hateful laugh—a laugh that haunted the men and nearly crazed them with anger.

One night some of the prisoners obtained a thin, strong wire. When the guard came into the compound, they slipped behind him, quickly tossed the wire across his throat, and with one swift, strong motion, cut off his head. Agipito caught the falling head as he rushed with the others to escape the compound.

Twenty miles through swamp and jungle the escaped prisoners tramped that night, headed in the direction of the American lines. Toward morning they sighted an American patrol.

"Hey, Joe!" someone called in a hoarse whisper. The patrol whirled with drawn guns and the crisp command to come out with hands high. Suddenly the patrol leader's eyes widened in horror. "What's that?" he demanded in disbelief. As he pointed to the object under Agipito's arm, Agipito looked down and for the first time realized that he still carried the hated Japanese guard's head.

Years passed. The war was over, and Agipito had settled down in Hawaii with his lovely wife Loretta and their six children... but the horror was not over. Night after night Agipito tossed sleeplessly as he relived the war. Often he was haunted by the sight of the blood spurting upward from the decapitated body of the Japanese guard as the headless form staggered before it fell. When he did sleep, his sleep was disturbed by violent nightmares that caused him to fight fiercely as he slept. So violent were his struggles that Loretta frequently sustained injury from them. Finally he had to make his bed in an isolated part of the house for the safety of those whom he loved. Always his hatred of the Japanese seethed within him.

Christmas 1956 had been almost upon them, and Agipito's family had little with which to celebrate. Agipito did not yet have his job operating the cranes, and the work in the mill below did not pay enough to cover all of his debts and his family's growing needs. He was too proud to ask for help from anyone.

"What are you having for Christmas dinner, Sextimo?" asked a thoughtless man working beside Agipito.

"You might kalua a dog," suggested a burly Japanese working across the big table from Agipito in a crude effort to jest.

To Agipito it was not funny. All the old hatred boiled up inside him. With a swift motion he seized a heavy iron tool and would have killed the Japanese had not the workmen beside him prevented it.

Agipito returned home angry, hurt, his old hatred for all Japanese flaming anew inside him. Suddenly there was a knock at the door. Agipito snatched it open to face two Japanese men, one of them bearing a box in his arms. Behind them were three Japanese girls.

"We are from the Reorganized Church of Jesus Christ of Latter Day Saints," announced the older man. "We have brought you a gift from the church." With that introduction the younger man handed Agipito a package of food, treats, and gifts for his family.

"For me?" gasped the startled Agipito. "Why for me? What do you want? I have no money."

"We want no money," Elder Nii explained. "We just learned that you might need a little help this Christmas, so we brought you this gift."

"But—but, what can I do in return?" stammered the puzzled Filipino. "And who did you say you are?"

There followed an explanation of the location of the church, assurance of their desire to help, and an invitation for the family to visit the church, especially during the series of meetings soon to be held. Sylvester Coleman, a seventy from Honolulu, would be the speaker.

When the Japanese elder and his four young friends took their leave, the amazed Filipino stood holding their gift and wondering. "Why," he mused, "would Japanese whom I hate so desperately, bring me, a Filipino, a gift to fill so great a need?"

Agipito reached down absentmindedly to grasp the lower section of his split door. As he turned to go inside, he glanced once more at the departing Japanese. The hatred that had so long burdened his heart began to melt away.

Christmas passed. The series of meetings opened, and Agipito was there. Each night he moved one row nearer to the front of the church until he reached the seat just back of the front one which was permanently occupied by the saintly Hawaiian matriarch of the congregation. There he sat night after night in rapt attention as he heard the gospel story presented by the seventy.

Agipito was baptized, and the joy that filled his body was indescribable. From that moment the nightmares were gone. Gone, too, was the hatred. There was no more fear. Now when his friends asked why he went to "that church" in which there were Japanese and Hawaiians, Haoles and Portuguese, Chinese and Hapa-haoles when he and his family were the only Filipinos, he answered, "Yes, but they are my brothers, and I love them. When they shake my hand, I know they love me."

The workday ended. Agipito climbed down from his cage with a sense of urgency hastening his movements. The hour was late—too late for him to take time to go home, eat supper, change, and get back to the church on time. But there was time to make it to prayer service just as he was to share his testimony. No, Agipito could never forget!

UNWARRANTED GARNISHEE

"Garnishee my wages, will they?" Agipito sputtered furiously. "I'll put these hands under the guillotine first and let them see what wages they can get!"

"Help him, please," Agipito's friend, Herbert, implored Delbert as he struggled with the distraught man on the doorstep.

"Come in, come in." Del grasped Agipito's arm firmly. "Tell me what has happened." My husband could see that whatever it was Agipito was distressed beyond his ability to cope with the situation.

"They took my car! They are going to garnishee my wages. They say I owe $425. I don't owe them anything! The paper says I'll have to appear in court at the capital. I can't go there. There's no way to go but by plane, and the fare will be more than $40. I'll cut off these hands. Then at least there will be money for my family." Agipito held his hands in front of him and stared as though he could already see the stubbs left from the sharp knife he operated daily to shear huge sheets of metal.

Had it not been for Herbert the hands might already have been gone. When the legal papers were served on Agipito instructing him to appear in court to answer charges of failure to pay and informing him his car was impounded and his wages were to be garnisheed, the insurance from such an injury was the only solution he could conceive for keeping his family fed. Working beside him Herbert had quickly perceived his intention, stopped the machinery, and insisted he see Delbert. Agipito knew Del as a minister but never thought of him as being either willing or able to help in such legal matters as this. In fact, he was accustomed to there being nothing anyone could do to "beat the law" for him and his people.

"It will not be necessary for you to cut off your hands," Del spoke reassuringly. "Just start at the beginning and tell me what this is all about."

Quickly the story spilled out. There had been a friend destitute of funds and with a family. Agipito's credit was good at the neighborhood grocer's so the friend was authorized to purchase groceries there for his family during his own emergency on Agipito's credit. The bill totaled more than $400 when the friend left town leaving Agipito to pay.

Agipito had signed a note and had arranged for monthly payment for the bill. One month he had been ill. He had asked for and received permission from the grocer to delay that payment. Now the legal papers said he had never made that payment nor any succeeding payment for the past eight months. The fine print on the note said that if one payment was missed the entire amount became immediately due with a penalty assessed. Apparently someone had seen an opportunity to make a few extra dollars. Now he was being charged with an amount greater than the original bill, and payment was demanded immediately. In fact, a collection agency now had the account and had obtained a legal order to possess the car, an ancient rattletrap worthless to anyone but to Agipito who knew how to keep it in operation to serve his family needs. In addition to this, his wages were to be garnisheed. Garnishee in the place he worked meant immediate dismissal.

"How many payments have you made?" Del asked.

"All of them!" Agipito asserted. "I have made every one of them!"

"Do you have your receipts?" Del inquired.

"I think so," Agipito hesitated. "I am not sure, but I think so."

"Then let's go see the grocer," Del suggested.

"It will not do any good," Agipito's friend volunteered. "We came by there on the way up. He says he has nothing to do with it."

"But you have been making your payments to the grocer?"

"Every one."

"Then, let's go see a lawyer."

"You know I cannot pay a lawyer," Agipito countered, angered and offended at the suggestion.

"You won't have to pay a lawyer. There must be someone in this town whose business it is to see that justice is done in situations like this." Del reached for the telephone.

It was the judge to whom Del and Agipito first told their story. He gave Del a few pointers about answering the charges made in the legal papers that had accompanied the possess and garnishee orders, then referred them to a lawyer retained by the county to give assistance in such situations.

"Herbert, you take Agipito home and gather up those receipts," Del instructed. "I'll type up this reply to the court. Come to the mission house as soon as you have the receipts, and we'll go see the lawyer."

Armed with all the receipts, Del and the men went to see the lawyer. Mr. Munoz read the papers, then Delbert's reply.

"If ever I get into trouble," the young lawyer smiled at Del, "I would like to have you on my side." There were instructions in delivering the legal reply and assurances of further assistance if it became necessary.

"Let's go to your employer," Del suggested when the legal reply was on its way. "I think he should know all about this."

So Del took Agipito to his boss, showed him the receipts,

and chronicled the course of events to that moment. "I'm afraid it's a racket someone has been getting away with," Del concluded. "But Agipito has done nothing to bring it on himself except to be ignorant of the justice available here."

"There is no need to worry," Mr. Hay assured them. "There will be no garnishee placed on this man's wages through this office." Agipito had long since begun to relax, and now reacted with relief that bordered on gaiety.

"Now to get the car released." Del was methodically clearing every issue. There was a long-distance call to the collection agency explaining the error.

"Even if this man did owe you," Del said, "taking that car away would do you no good. It's worthless to anyone but Agipito. Holding it you only make it difficult for him to pay his other bills. But he does not owe you." Del was emphatic. "He has every receipt. If you have a grievance, it is against the groceryman who has been collecting the money regularly."

The next day the car was released. An apologetic collection agency official called to have Del and Agipito go with him to the grocer where, confronted with the receipts, the grocer confessed to his "error." Agipito returned to work.

"What if he had cut off his hands?" Del mused. "How desperately we need to be rid of ignorance, opportunism, and injustice even in this promised land!"

TAMA, THE CHURCH, AND THE KAHUNA

"Sister Benes! Are you all right, Sister Benes?" Delbert was a little out of breath. It had taken a few minutes to drive from the mission house on the mountainside to the fern garden beside the bay. Once there, he parked his car, and with a hurried, "I'll run ahead," to me he ran the length of the rugged lava path that passed between the rough-hewn, tin-roofed cottages set in a tangle of tropical undergrowth beneath the huge banyan trees and palms that skirted the area. Several times, where the *lilikoi* vines hung heavy with fruit, he bent low to avoid the hard, yellow spheres. Chickens housed in the crude pens beside the path clamored fearfully against the wire walls of their enclosures as he ran by. A little *poi* dog barked excitedly and nipped at his heels. Even the game cocks, penned individually in carefully hidden stacks beside some of the houses, betrayed their hiding places by their screeches of disapproval of this hasty intrusion into their cloistered serenity. In one bound he cleared the three rough steps that led to the crudely banistered porch that stretched across the front of the house and now spoke through the open door. There was no answer.

"Sister Benes!" Del's call was louder this time and tinged with a sense of urgency. Tama had sounded strange, as though she were in deep trouble when she had telephoned for him to come minutes before. "Sister Benes! May I come in?" Unless it was absolutely necessary he did not wish to cross the threshold unbidden.

A tall, lean, disheveled woman shuffled through the doorway directly opposite the outer door in which Delbert stood and stopped just inside the tiny living room where she leaned heavily on the wall.

Del had never seen Tama like this. Always before her simple clothing had been clean and neat; her sleek black hair, pulled tightly into a bun at the back of her head, had accentuated her classic features making her almost beautiful. Her snapping brown eyes, now clouded and bloodshot, had always spoken their welcome in terms of intelligence, happiness, and peace.

"Tama!" I had come into the doorway to stand beside Del. "Tama! What has happened to you? What is the matter?"

"I am drunk!" The woman spoke flatly and finally as though this was, for her, the end of everything.

"But how... why... what has happened?" Del was clearly puzzled. For months he had thought he knew this woman whom suddenly he seemed to know so little.

There were the early days of their acquaintanceship. Her husband came alone to the church to see whether this gospel message he had heard was really worthwhile. Weeks of teaching followed in their home—not the usual six or eight cottage meetings but many more because the need and desire to know were so great. There was baptism. Then came the period of church attendance during which the radiance of the Master shone from her face and the face of her husband.

There had also been weeks of visiting the hospital almost daily when Dola, their little one, was there. During the time we visited in the home we had noticed that the little girl never smiled. In fact, she hardly responded to her environment at all. When she was pleased there was sometimes a brief grimace that pulled the corners of her mouth straight out momentarily, then left the face as passive as ever. Although nearly two years of age, she could neither stand alone nor walk.

Because of my training in the field of nutrition, I thought I recognized a nutritional deficiency in the child and asked about her food. Milk was her diet. Milk was all she wanted, her mother asserted, so milk was all she got. It was then that the welfare agency had been called in and the child had been hospitalized.

In less than a week the passive face began to come alive. Soon the corners of her mouth began to curve into a smile. Then came the wonderful day when she walked! Del and I had shared this happy moment with Tama and her husband and with them had thanked God for the food and care that were making her well. There were, of course, the final weeks of recuperation with frequent visits to the children's ward.

We had shared hours of prayer and consultation when Tama and Juan had come to ask whether they should let the doctor perform the operation that he had recommended after the birth of their seventh child. Childbearing, the doctor had said, was threatening Tama's health and her ability to care for the children she already had. And now this! How could she be drunk? She who had loved her new life in Christ so much!

"I am drunk!" Tama spoke with a lurch of her head that seemed to push the words past her thick tongue.

One look around the usually immaculate though sparsely furnished house indicated that she had been drunk for some time. The place was a mess. Mud caked the doorways; dirt littered the floor; dishes were piled high on the dirty table from which the leftover stew and rice from some previous meal had not been removed. The baby, who had just passed his first birthday, lay crying uncared for and unnoticed on the bed.

"We see," Del replied simply. "You get some sleep now, and we'll come back tomorrow when you can talk."

I washed the drunk woman's hands and face and prepared her for bed. There she lay whimpering like a lost child. The baby was bathed, changed, fed, and tucked snugly into his bed. Together Del and I swept and scrubbed and washed and dusted until the bare little house shone as usual.

When all was in order, Del made a brief stop at Brother Benes' place of employment to inform him of the situation at home and returned to the mission house for the night.

Early the next morning we returned to the cottage by the sea. Tama was sober now . . . and repentant.

"Do you want to tell us about it?" Del inquired.

"It was my mother." She spoke clearly now, but with an intensity that sometimes caused her voice to tremble. "You see, I am an alcoholic." She paused as if to let the full impact of the words sink deeply into our minds. Then she told how she had been freed from her desire for liquor when she first came to know the church of Jesus Christ.

It is the custom that when an island baby reaches one year of age, the family celebrates with a *luau,* complete from *Kalua* pig and sweet potatoes to plenty of alcoholic beverages.

"You were at our *luau.*" Tama searched her callers' faces for confirmation. "You know that we did not allow any liquor to be served."

Because there had been no liquor Tama's mother had been very angry. She was angry, too, because this seventh child would be the last. She accused her daughter of having cheated God because long ago the *Kahuna* had predicted that she would bear eight.

Yesterday when she was drunk Tama had repeatedly mumbled something about having displeased God because she could not have an eighth child, so Del interrupted her story to inquire of the trembling woman, "Did God tell you that you were to have eight children?"

"No." Tama was almost startled by the thought.

"Did you not ask God about the operation?" he gently persisted.

"Yes. Yes, we did!" and a trace of a smile touched her eyes as she began to comprehend.

"Then why should the prediction of the *Kahuna* concern you?"

With a long sigh of relief the woman returned to her narrative.

"And so she insisted that I go drink with her. It was the least I could do, she declared, since I had cheated her out of both a proper celebration for her seventh grandchild and out of any at all for an eighth." Tama took a long breath and dropped her head in her hands. Wearily she told of how the unworthy mother had begged and threatened and accused until finally she had succumbed. One drink led to another, as is always true with alcoholics. Finally, in desperation, she had called Del.

A long, earnest conversation followed as Del ministered to the woman. Finally he asked, "Tama, may I see your Bible?" When she had brought it, he questioned, "Do you mind if I mark in it a scripture that I want you to remember always?"

Having received her permission, he read aloud to her as he carefully underlined the words, "For I am come to set a man at variance against his father and the daughter against her mother ... and a man's foes shall be they of his own household. *He who loveth father and mother more than me, is not worthy of me....* He who seeketh to save his life shall lose it: and he who loseth his life for my sake shall find it."

A MATTER OF CARING

"School tomorrow!" I commented cheerfully as I drove toward Kimiville with a car filled with children. Twice each Sunday, before morning and evening services, both the pastor and Delbert drove or sent their cars to the settlement of ugly, unpainted barracks and gathered all the children—and adults too—who would come with them to the church.

"I cannot go to school tomorrow," lamented Piadora.

"And why not?" I questioned.

"Because I have sores all over my legs, and teacher said not to come back without having them doctored and covered," explained the unhappy child.

I glanced down at the beautiful child in the too big, badly faded muu muu snuggling close to my side. "Let me see," I suggested.

Piadora lifted the long, loose fitting dress and disclosed a mass of impetigo such as I had never seen. Well trained in suppressing the evidence of shock in even the most shocking situations, I asked matter-of-factly, "Mother will doctor them for you tonight, will she not?"

"No! Mother says she will just let them take me to the hospital tomorrow. But I do not want to go to the hospital.... I want to go to school!" The child's voice betrayed the tears that threatened at the hopelessness of her situation.

I said nothing more of Piadora's problem as I went from door to door unloading the car's burden of children and calling out "See you next Sunday" to each as they left.

Finally they were all gone but Piadora, her sister Shirley, and the girls' four brothers.

"Tell you what," I said. "I will ask your mother to let you stay with me tonight if you would like, and we will doctor those sores so you can go to school tomorrow. Would you like that?"

"Oh, Sister Smith! *Would* you?" The little girl could scarcely contain her excitement.

"Okay. Out with you," I said, stopping the car in front of the next-to-last barracks in the circle near the entrance to the settlement.

"You are coming too, are you not?" asked Piadora anxiously.

"I am right behind you, dear," I reassured her.

Inside the long, low building in which the children lived, the meager furnishings were neatly arranged, and the house was clean. The drabness of the unpainted walls was relieved by pictures cut from calendars and those brought home from church by the children. In one corner sat a beautiful monstera which evidently received the loving and competent care of someone in the home.

I knew very well the large, handsome, poorly dressed woman who greeted me as I entered the house. For months Del and I had been trying to teach this mother a better way of life than she knew. Once when she and her children had come to our home to talk of her problems she seemed to come close to understanding the message of Christ. But always her old habits seemed to drag her back from the brink of perception—a perception which could have launched her into the new life to which Delbert had come to lead her.

Del had first met the family when the children had come to the Christmas program at the church at the invitation of the pastor. Danny, Jr., was ten then and felt the weight of responsibility that was his for three little brothers and sisters.

Early in the service Kenneth, the youngest, had gone fast asleep, and Junior had tried to hold him on his lap. Seeing the brave struggle the valiant boy was having with his little brother, I had brought a blanket from the car and made a bed for the little one. Though relieved to be rid of his burden, Junior was hesitant at first to trust a complete stranger to care for his little brother. The bed was, therefore, made close to Junior's feet on the floor beside the back seat of the church so he could enjoy the service, assured that his brother was safe.

Del knew the children's father well also. Each week he visited the clean-cut Filipino in his hospital room at Puuamaile. The big, beautiful hospital had been built high on the mountainside above the town to care for the needs of the many in the area who had tuberculosis. As Danny, Sr., looked down over the city to where his family lived, his heart ached to be with them to give them the love and care which he knew they needed so much. Occasionally he was permitted to visit them for a day, and what a day of rejoicing it always was for the children!

This night the mother greeted me cordially and inquired, as mothers do, about the behavior of her children at church.

"Piadora tells me that she cannot go to school tomorrow because of the sores on her legs," I said.

"Yes," answered the woman passively. "Seems like they are always covered with sores. There is just no way to get rid of the fleas under the house, and that is where they always want to play."

"Would it be all right with you if I took Piadora home with me tonight to doctor her sores? Maybe she could stay all week until they are entirely well."

I had scarcely finished and the mother had had no time to reply when David spoke up eagerly. "Look!" The boy tugged fiercely at his faded jeans. "See . . . I have sores too!"

The lifted jeans revealed a mass of impetigo similar to that which covered his sister's legs. "May I go with you too?"

"If your mother says you may," I agreed.

Although it was late, I knew that our family doctor would be at his little hospital or would come if he was called. The venerable Japanese gentleman was not only competent but compassionate as well. So we went home laden with the proper medicines and instructed in the care of the sores. Dr. Ota had even injected antibiotics into Piadora because of the advanced stage of putrefaction on the surface of her legs and the extensive area of her body that the infection covered.

Next morning we took the children to school and watched Piadora skip happily toward the classroom door, her legs swathed in bandages. David ran close beside her with similar bandages, though his did not show. Deeply moved, we lifted our hearts in prayer to God, who we knew cared even more than did we. We prayed that the message of his kingdom might soon penetrate the hearts and minds of all mankind and that the sin, poverty, and distress that had robbed their mother of her ability to care anymore could soon be eliminated from all the earth. The love that we felt for those children caught in a wave of circumstances they could not control, for their erring mother sick in spirit, for their father sick in body, and for the many families like them did not end, and our yearning for the coming kingdom knew no respite. "How does one *really* serve his Lord, Jesus the Christ?" we asked, as we drove from the school toward the mission house.

THE UNCERTAIN PROSTITUTE

"Sister Smith! Sister Smith! It is Sister Smith!" called the children excitedly as I approached the long, low, unpainted barracks home.

"Come in, Sister Smith!" David and Piadora fairly pulled me into the neat living room.

"I will get Mother!" volunteered David.

Soft strains from a ukulele were drifting from the bedroom just off the living room near the front. They accompanied a melodious female voice, but the words of the song she was singing were slightly garbled by the influence of the wine that had come from the bottle which now lay on the floor with its neck protruding from under the curtain that served as a bedroom door.

As the flimsy curtain fluttered with the passing of David's lithe body into the room, it was evident that had it not been for the liquor, neither the children nor I would have been inside the house. There had been other times when Mrs. B. had had a customer. Then the door had been securely barred against them all. There had even been Sunday mornings when the children had been locked outside before they had had time to wash and dress in clean clothing.

"Sister Smith will take you as you are," their mother had assured them. "She will understand."

Prone on the bed beside the buxom woman lay a man sensuously caressing her body as she sang her love songs and strummed her ukulele.

"Mama. Sister Smith is here. Come!" urged David as he tugged at his mother's arm.

"Oh! Oh! Oh-h-h!" moaned the woman. Then to her companion, "Wait a minute."

It took a moment for her to disentangle herself from her customer's embrace. Then she came, staggering through the flimsy curtain clutching ashamedly at her even more flimsy gown in an effort to make it cover her generous bosom.

The clouded brown eyes must once have been very beautiful. Even now there was a trace of glory left in the disheveled black hair, the deeply tanned skin, the nearly perfect features. Her voice, when she spoke, still hinted of low music, marred now by the thickness of her tongue and the intensity of her embarrassment.

"Oh, Sister Smith!" The dark eyes shifted evasively away from mine, "I do not like for you to see me like this!"

Looking at her I remembered the hours of loving ministry we had given this poor woman. These had included hours spent in the judge's office and with welfare personnel as Del had joined forces with those professionals in an effort to correct the situation which existed in this home. There had been hours of hope when Mrs. B. had seemed to comprehend what God had in mind for her and had determined to let his love work in her so that she might walk in his way. There had been times when she had come to church and into our home with her children and had found real joy with the Saints.

But the hours of hope and progress seemed always to give way to hours of disappointment as those moments of inspiration and resolution were overwhelmed by the old way of life which, it seemed, she could not bring herself to abandon. This was one of those heartbreaking disappointments, and I could hardly choke back the tears as I replied pleadingly, "Mrs. B., if you never *got* like this, I could never see you like this!"

Then hurrying on to the purpose for which I had come I explained, "I came to see if the children could go with us this afternoon. We are going to pick guava, and I thought they might like to come along. We will bring them back after supper."

"Sure . . . sure . . . take them along!" Anxiety spilled into Mrs. B.'s voice as she fidgeted nervously with her scanty garment.

Gleefully the six happy children fairly tumbled into our car while their mother pulled aside the flimsy curtain and staggered back to her bedroom. As I closed the car door, I again heard sounds of the ukelele and of a once beautiful voice, thickened now with wine, chanting an ancient love song.

A TIME FOR CHOOSING

"If something should happen to me, will you take care of my children?"

It was a male voice on the telephone. The low, terse words sounded as though they came from one who had finally gained control of himself after a long, hard battle. As he finished there was something in his pleading voice of the calm that follows turbulence in the words, "I know they love you, and you love them."

"Who is this?" I asked. Then, as understanding dawned, "Is this Mr. B.?"

"Yes. This is Mr. B.," came the weary reply.

"Of course, we would do anything we could for your children," I answered, then drew a deep breath as the impact of what that could mean struck my consciousness.

"I think I could get someone else to take the boys, but would you take the girls for yours?" The anxious man wanted to be certain there was no misunderstanding. This commitment was to be for keeps.

I paused long enough to fill my lungs full of air to try to make certain that the fear which struck my heart did not show through my voice. It was apparent that the man on the other end of the line had made a decision, one that he was sure could cost his life. When I was sure of my voice again, I replied calmly, "Yes, Mr. B., if you want us to, we will be glad to take your girls. But what is the matter?"

"I have given her the choice—him or me." There was no life in the voice.

"But surely . . ."

"I do not think it will be me," he interrupted, "and I have been sick so long I don't know whether I could make a home for the children or whether I will have a chance to try."

I knew very well what the man meant. Only a few days earlier there had been the excited little voice on the telephone pleading, "Brother Smeeth, Brother Smeeth, Mama says to come quick!"

We hurriedly piled our own small children into the car and drove across town to the weather-beaten slum home from which the child had run to the public telephone to call.

With a quick, "Stay here in the car," to the children, Del ran up to the closed door of the barrack home and knocked.

"Stop," came the startling command of an angry male voice inside. "Go away, or I will shoot!"

Ignoring the command or the presence of the man, Del called, "Mrs. B."

"I said go away or I will shoot," the man inside growled.

"I came," Del said, "because Mrs. B. asked for me. I will not leave until she sends me away."

The voice inside rose in a frenzy of profanity punctuating repeated threats of murder.

Del never moved. "Mrs. B.," he called without a hint of fear or intent to retreat, "open the door."

"Oh, no, Brother Smith." It was the first time Del was even sure that she was there. "Please go away. It is all right now."

"Are you sure?" Del questioned.

Again the male voice rose in a crescendo of profanity, and what sounded like a brief scuffle ensued. The woman's voice came again, this time with real assurance. "Yes, Brother Smith. It *is* all right now. Please go away."

"If you are sure you want me to go." Del hesitated to leave without seeing that Mrs. B. was safe.

"I am sure. Please go." she urged. "He has been drinking."

Del had driven reluctantly away. But he had returned the next day to see that it was really all right in the B. home. There he had met the tall, surly man, less belligerent without his liquor. A relative of their father's, the children called him "Uncle." It was apparent that he meant to take his place in this home to stay.

And so when Mr. B. returned from the tuberculosis hospital—this time, he hoped, to stay—he found his place usurped. Because of his love for his wife and family, he—knowing well what the outcome might be—gave her the choice. But Del never knew whether it was by her free choice or by the force of the threats of the "Uncle" that she chose the surly intruder.

We did not, however, have to take the girls or the boys. Mr. B. was able to make a home for all his children. With the help of governmental agencies and the encouagement of Del, who helped him overcome his fears and to follow the necessary procedure, he moved his family to a beautiful housing development home and there cared for their needs as only a loving father can.

Mrs. B.? We never saw her again, but we still prayed that some way, some day she might yet repent, return to her family, and become the beautiful woman God wanted her to be.

MAMASAN'S MAGNIFICENT GIFT

I picked my way carefully along the rough lava path that wound through the neatly trimmed California grass, past the lichee tree with its nearly ripe fruit, and on to the lean-to shed that served as laundry and bath for the family that called this handmade cottage home. Carefully lifting the *lilikoi* vine out of the way so that I would not damage it, I stepped onto the smoothly polished lava stones that were the floor of the lean-to and called to Masako.

While I waited for an invitation to enter the house, I noticed the neat pile of clothes waiting to be laundered at one end of Masako's lean-to. I noted the ingenious way Hachiro had used the left-over tin from the roof to fashion a door for the *furo*. My curiosity about how the steam bath was really operated almost caused me to cross the threshold and peer uninvited through the door.

Masako's soft call of welcome interrupted my survey of

the lean-to's interior. I moved quickly across the lava floor toward the covered ledge alongside the house which I must traverse to enter the family's living quarters. I had given the big red mongrel chained to the porch a familiar pat of greeting and started into the house when I saw Mamasan, Masako's mother, coming toward me smiling and bowing profusely.

Between her gnarled hands that were extended palms-together in greeting, Mamasan pressed a small brown paper bag which she was obviously offering as she murmured something over and over in Japanese. I understood her *"Arigato gozaimas."* "Thank you" is a word one soon learns in any language. But why, I wondered, the profuse thanks and the proffered gift?

Placing my palms together in an answering gesture of greeting I returned Mamasan's bow and smiled as I waited. Shuffling forward in the little trotting gait with which I was now familiar and bowing low at every step, Mamasan crossed the valley that separated the raised living area from the sleeping rooms. I noticed that the unpainted floorboards were polished smooth with much scrubbing and the constant shuffling of slippered feet.

When she reached the open doorway where I was standing, Mamasan pressed the parcel into my hands. Inside there were apples! Why would Mamasan, who had so little, spend her precious money for apples in this land of tropical fruit where apples were so expensive? And why did she present them to me with such ceremony?

Now it was my turn to bow and murmur *"Arigato gozaimas."* Feeling keenly my inability to communicate adequately with Mamasan in the only language the dear old woman knew, I accepted the gift, bowed low again, and waited for Masako to come to my rescue with explanations of her mother's behavior.

"They are apples," said Masako softly, her lovely smile lighting her still young and beautiful face, though the eldest of her own three children was nearly as large as she. "Apples for the children. Mamasan wants you to have them. It is so little for all your husband has done for us."

And then I understood. I had been feeding the baby that day when Lynn came to the door all out of breath. She came every day to the door to ask politely, "May I practice my lesson on your piano now?" And every day I assured her that I was glad to have a piano on which one with such talent could learn to use that talent well. But on this day Lynn was not thinking of the piano or of her practice.

"Can Brother Smith come quickly?" she asked breathlessly. "Mamasan is bleeding, and the doctors cannot stop it." Del went quickly with the frightened little girl. First he took her home, and then he dashed to the hospital where Mamasan lay, her life slowly ebbing as the nasal hemorrhage flowed on unchecked. Already there had been one transfusion, but the family was poor and transfusions cost money. No one in the family was physically able to replace the blood the doctors had used. There had been tuberculosis. Even now Masako's brother, Mamasan's son, was in the hospital suffering from the disease.

Carefully Del explained to Masako that which he wanted Mamasan to know about the God who loved her and made her and could make her well. Faithfully Masako translated the message to Mamasan. Together they told of the way God had chosen to bring about such healing ministry by the laying on of the elders' hands. They explained how Del had been called of God to perform such ministry. Then Masako asked, "Mamasan, do you want Brother Smith to pray for you?"

Tears filled the faded eyes of the good woman who so long had known only the god of Buddha—a god who demanded the benign acceptance of suffering as the stuff of which life is made, a god who ruled without consideration of any person's need, a god who demanded the extinction of all personality by self-sacrifice, contemplation, and suppression of all passion. The gray head nodded assent on its pillow as the deep furrows that crossed her weathered face in great profusion seemed to relax in childlike faith in the new God she had just come to know.

The anointing was quickly performed. The prayer was soon finished. The hemorrhage stopped. Mamasan rested quietly.

But Del did not rest; he went to the hospital laboratory. "I hear you need blood," he said, "to replace that which you used for Mamasan in Room 201. Will mine do?"

And so there was no bill for blood for the family to pay, and Mamasan felt that the fresh blood that ran through her veins was that of the young seventy who had told her about a God who loved her, who had created her, and who had made her well.

AMI'S TRIUMPH

Del was first introduced to Roy Gay by Miguel De la Cruz, principal of the Waikea Kai Elementary School which the Gay children attended. The big Hawaiian had approached Elder De la Cruz when he had learned that he belonged to a Latter Day Saint church that was not Mormon. Roy was troubled. Six months or so previously he and his family had been baptized into the Mormon Latter-day Saints' church, thrilled by the principles of the gospel they had been taught and willing to go all the way with the Christ of the Restoration.

As the Gay family attended classes in the church, however, they began to hear of new practices and principles that troubled them. When they asked why they had not been taught them before baptism, they were told they were not ready for them then. When it became apparent that some of the teachings included practices that Roy considered immoral, he fairly exploded and went to talk to Elder De la Cruz.

"He has so many questions," Brother De la Cruz told Del, "I just cannot answer them all. Maybe you can help him."

"I'll surely try." Del was enthusiastic.

Night after night, after his other work was finished, he joined the big Hawaiian in the guardhouse at the entrance to the wharf at Hilo Bay. The night hours sped by as they talked of the Restoration and of Christ's mission and intent for the earth. The seventy produced scripture after scripture and document after document to negate the teachings that had disillusioned Roy.

"What else do you teach?" the Hawaiian asked frequently. "What will I learn if I come into the church that you are not telling me now?"

"Nothing," Del assured him. "Nothing that you do not find right here in the Scriptures," and he patted the three books reverently.

With renewed hope Roy began to bring his family to church. There he questioned intently every idea presented, every statement made that seemed at all different from that which he had believed throughout his life. Finally he apologized for his interrogations.

"You must be disgusted with me for seeming to heckle you so," he said one day. "But I have to know! I got burned, once, and I cannot let it happen again."

"Don't worry," Del encouraged him. "We understand and are more than happy to have you ask every question that comes into your mind."

Soon thereafter Roy asked for baptism.

The day came when his wife Ami also decided to dedicate her life to the Christ. Her son Charles asked to join with her in her dedication. It was a perfect day in the tropics. Del filled the church car to overflowing with young people added to his own growing family for the early morning trip across the Saddle Road that led through the Pohakuloa military training ground between the mountains, Mauna Loa and Mauna Kea, to the Kona side of the island where the Gays had moved when Roy went to work for Kona Inn. It would be the first baptism of the church in Kona waters, the old-time Saints had informed the seventy.

"Do you know a good spot along the shore for the baptism...maybe an inlet or sheltered cove?" Del asked Roy.

"I think we had better get an onshore pool," the Hawaiian suggested hesitantly.

"Do you know of one?" Del was disappointed but did not want to be obstinate. This was too joyful an occasion to let anything mar it.

"One of the neighbors down the road has a big fishpond that might do," Roy suggested.

"Let's go see it as soon as the morning service is over."

Benches and chairs were set out under the trees that separated the rough beach from the Gays' dooryard. With the gentle swishing of the waves on the shore for a background, the service got under way. Del directed the service, led the singing, and preached to the appreciative little group. There was a picnic lunch under the trees, and preparations began for the baptisms.

"Is the fishpond suitable?" I asked.

"Hardly," Del replied, wrinkling his nose to indicate the presence of offensive odor. "It's green and slimy!"

"We would have to institute a new form of baptism, too," rejoined Roy. "Ami just would not fit." He laughed as he pulled his tall, slender wife to his side for an affectionate hug.

"Now what?" I persisted.

"There's a beautiful cove just off the road a few hundred yards down the way." Del was enthusiastic. "The waves are coming in pretty high, but it is beautiful!"

Roy looked at his pretty wife, and they exchanged meaningful glances that neither of us could interpret. "It *is* a pretty spot," Roy agreed with reservation.

"Do you have a preference as to who will be baptized first?" Del questioned.

"Oh, let Charles be first," Ami responded almost too quickly.

Del looked up from his note sheet briefly, but asked no questions.

Just off the narrow highway that circled the Big Island, the little group filed through the opening in the tropical foliage made by some ancient lava flow that had not yet given in to the encroachment of vegetation. It was like stepping through a magic doorway from the dusty highway to the surf-washed shore of the Pacific. High waves rolled in to break gently on the almost sandless beach. Lava boulders had been worn smooth by centuries of waves washing over the area, giving it the appearance of a pebbly beach being seen under a microscope. Footing was treacherous, and the big Hawaiian stayed close to help me keep my balance with our youngest in my arms. Del took Ami and Charles to the very edge of the water. The rest gathered close in. Even then the pounding of the waves and the swish of the water made hearing difficult.

There was a song and a prayer. Del talked about the significance of the covenant that Ami and Charles were making, the historic nature of the act about to be performed in Kona waters, and the joy of heaven at the response of men. Then he led Charles into the water. In spite of the big waves, to find water deep enough for the immersion required quite a long walk. "When the big one comes, just let me lift you up," the seventy instructed Charles. "Then when it has passed, I will immerse you in the quieter waters between the waves." From the shore the waiting congregation could see the raised hand as the pronouncement of baptism was offered though no words could be heard.

With the immersion completed, Del escorted the happy boy, smiling broadly, back to the shore and took Ami by the hand. Standing beside Roy, I heard a sound and turned to hear what he was saying. There stood the big man poised on the rocks, every muscle tensed as though he were ready for flight right into the ocean. His eyes were glued to Ami and Del as he watched them intently.

Ami walked confidently by Del's side, her hand in his, to the place of baptism. As she turned to face the congregation, her eyes sought out those of her husband and she smiled happily as some precious communication passed between them. I watched as the tense muscles relaxed.

When the immersion was completed, Roy turned to me. "I did not know whether Ami could go through with it," he explained. "You see, she is deathly afraid of the ocean. Since her brother drowned in it, she has not set foot in it until now. Look at her!" he exclaimed fervently. "There is no fear there now, is there?"

"No fear at all!" I agreed. "How does the Good Book say it? 'Perfect love casteth out all fear'!"

His heart filled with love, the big Hawaiian reached out to take his wife's hand. He wrapped her in the robe he had brought for her and stood with bowed head as Del asked God's benediction on that which had transpired. The waves of the incoming tide lapped at their feet and swished away, adding their own benediction to that moment of love.

A TREASURE CHEST FOR GIVING

"Ronald, you have won! You've won! Daddy, Ronnie won!"

It was Alan's jubilant shout that brought the seventy up from his office early that Christmas Eve.

"Won what? What is it that is causing such a celebration?"

"Daddy," five-year-old Ronald was eager to be the first to tell him, "I won the treasure chest. You know—the big box of toys in the drugstore window. The man from the drugstore just called and told Mother."

"Now, what do you know about that! Well, let's go get them and see what is there."

Three excited boys scrambled down the stairs and tumbled into the car parked under the house. Baby Karen, catching the thrill of the others, toddled toward the door and stood precariously near the edge of the top step of the long flight of stairs to the ground.

"Here, little one, you help Mother get supper ready before our company comes," I cajoled as I plucked the child back from danger and cuddled her fondly.

What a treasure chest it turned out to be! The children,

breathless with excitement, squealed with delight as each item was revealed. There were games and toys of every description. From the huge pink and blue teddy bear to the big battery-powered bulldozer with all its attachments to the parade of American presidents, every piece was truly a treasure.

"Ronnie," I said to the happy little boy surrounded by the heap of toys, "you know the Gays are coming to spend Christmas with us. Their daddy has not had much work this fall, and they will have very few presents except for that which we can give them. I really believe that God let you have the treasure chest to see how far he could trust you with his gifts—to see how much you would be willing to share."

Ronnie smiled back. "Mama," he said reassuringly, "there will be something for every one of them. And there will be something for Larry, too. What should I give Larry?"

"He has so many toys," it was Del who spoke now, "I don't think Larry will need another."

"But I want him to have one," persisted Ronnie. "I think I'll just let him have his choice."

"I'll run and get him," cried Alan excitedly, and he was off like a streak to bring his best friend from next door to see the wondrous gifts and to choose one for himself.

"I'll take this one," announced Larry, reaching for the splendid bulldozer with its batteries, lights, equipment. I looked at Del. He swallowed hard. Would Ronnie be equal to the moment?

"Okay," said Ronnie, happily assembling the equipment. "Mama, Daddy, Larry gets the bulldozer." We breathed great sighs of relief as we smiled our approval.

"Now what will we give the Gays?" Ronnie was already planning the other gifts to be given away. "Barbara is too big for most of the things," he mused. "I guess she'll have to have the teddy bear."

I gasped. The teddy bear was so beautiful! I had secretly hoped Ronnie would keep it, for it would look so pretty on his bed or on Karen's.

"Now let's see. There are Charles and the twins and Lani."

Soon a beautiful and appropriate gift had been designated for each of the children.

The remaining toys began to look like the leftovers on a bargain counter by comparison to those to be given away.

"Are you sure this is the way you want it?" I asked, feeling that I may have been too convincing in my little speech about God's purpose.

"I'm sure," Ronnie answered without hesitation. "Let's wrap the presents for the Gays."

RECONCILIATION

"Brother Smith," the voice that trembled on the telephone was barely audible. "I will not be able to be baptized tomorrow after all."

Sensing the trauma Takeo felt, Delbert knew it would be better if they could talk face-to-face. "Would it be all right if Sylvester and I came down to see you?" he asked solicitously.

"Oh, yes. Do come," the troubled little Buddhist answered eagerly.

"Now what do you suppose that is all about?" my husband mused as he turned to the other seventy with whom he had had the pleasure of working for the past few weeks and who was a guest at the mission house. "Takeo says she cannot be baptized Sunday. What do you suppose has happened? I am sure her husband has given his permission."

"Why don't we go find out?" Sylvester suggested.

It had been several months since Takeo had first been introduced to Christ's church by a nurse friend with whom she worked. The problems associated with living had grown almost too much for the tiny Japanese. "You are on the verge of a nervous breakdown," the doctor had cautioned. "You had better make the necessary adjustments to avert it before it is too late."

Just what those "necessary adjustments" were would have been hard to define. She had to keep on working. Her children needed money to continue their education. Her husband had to travel to keep his job. And her aged father was her responsibility, even though he was often irrational and extremely difficult to handle.

"Come with me to the church," Kay had invited her. "Hatsumi took me there when I could not see my way through my problems. You will find the Christ a real help in time of trouble," she testified of her own new faith.

Takeo was just getting acquainted with the Christ when Sylvester Coleman came to hold a series of meetings at the yellow frame church on Ululani Street. Eagerly she had listened to the wonderful story of a God who lived and loved and ministered to the needs of his children.

"I have so much to learn," she said one day. "Could you come to my home to teach me?"

It was an invitation for which the seventies had prayed. "When will it be most convenient for us to come?"

The date and time were set. After their first session at the spacious white frame home of the Okados, Takeo made another request. "You keep telling me to pray," she said, "and I do not know how to pray. Will you teach me, please?"

Joyfully the two ministers taught the humble Buddhist to pray to her Father, the God whom Buddha could only contemplate but whom the Christ now revealed to her.

Now, before they left the mission house on their errand to the Okado home, they paused to offer their own prayer for understanding, discernment, and direction. It was useless to try to anticipate Takeo's need, but they could pray that their ministry would be equal to it.

Nestled at the base of Halai Hill, an old cinder cone from some ancient volcanic eruption, the Okado home overlooked an expanse of lawn framed by gorgeous plantings of shrubs and flowers and kept beautifully by patient effort. As the ministers approached the large glassed-in front porch, they viewed with appreciation the tropical plantings with which it was hung. The orchids among them never ceased to fascinate Del.

When she met them at the door, Takeo's face was white and drawn. She, who had been so happy in anticipation of her baptism, now barely smiled as she welcomed her guests. There was no reason to waste time in formalities so, with complete candor, Del asked, "What is it, Takeo? Why can you not be baptized?"

"Because I wronged someone years ago and I cannot make it right." Her voice almost broke into a sob, and she regained her composure with difficulty. "I have been reading the Scriptures, and they say that if I want to come to the Lord, I have to be reconciled to those I have wronged first. The one I wronged does not live here anymore. I cannot ask her to forgive me before tomorrow, so I cannot be baptized."

"Where does she live?" The seventies were not about to give up so easily on something that meant so much to the diminutive nurse.

Takeo named the town across the Island. "But I do not

know her address. It has been so long since I have seen her!" In spite of her despair, the very presence of the ministers seemed to give her hope.

"Would she have a telephone?" Del suggested.

"Perhaps." Takeo brightened. "Would it be all right to do it by phone?" She had somehow presumed that reconciliation would need to be done face-to-face.

"Why do you not try?" Sylvester encouraged her.

* * * * *

Again the telephone rang at the mission house. Del recognized Takeo's voice immediately. "Did you contact your friend?" he questioned.

"I did," came the happy reply, "and do you know, she had forgotten what I did to wrong her! Here it had bothered me all these years, and she did not even remember!"

"Good!" my husband said thankfully.

"But I still cannot be baptized tomorrow!" Again the joy went out of the woman's voice. "I remembered another whom I wronged, and she is dead. I can never ask her forgiveness."

"That, Takeo, is why Christ died for us," Del explained gently. "There are many things that we cannot undo once they are done. If we truly repent and ask him in faith he has promised to do for us that which we would but cannot do. You do believe he has all power, do you not?"

"Oh, yes. You have taught me that well, and I do believe." Takeo once again had hope.

"And we have taught you how to pray," Del reminded her. "If you will tell him all about it and ask him to lift your burden, he will do it gladly. Do you want us to come to pray with you?"

"Oh, no!" The joy was returning to Takeo's voice. "I am sure I can do it alone."

A radiant Japanese dressed in white presented herself at the water's edge when it came her turn to be baptized the next day. The joy of new birth shone from her face as she stepped from the water into her new life with the Christ—her ever present, ever powerful Lord of forgiveness, light, and love.

BRIDGE OF LOVE

Soon after Takeo's baptism, she and Kay invited Delbert to meet two young schoolteachers whom they hoped he could teach about the Christ.

The first night the girls embarrassed their hostesses painfully by asking, "Why should we believe in Jesus Christ more than in Buddha?"

"Because he is the Son of God," Del answered.

"Who is God?" Leiko questioned.

"The Bible says that he..." Del began a little less confidently. He knew he was telling the truth, but he was already beginning to see where this conversation was going to lead. The usual answers would not suffice.

"Why should we believe the Bible?" Leiko interrupted defiantly. "It has nothing to do with us!" Leiko was apparently spokesman for the two Buddhists with whom Takeo and Kay had hoped to share their newfound faith.

"I see how you can feel that way," Del responded sympathetically. He recalled the popular interpretations of the Scripture that made God too small to include the world in his providence.

"Let's . . . let us," he corrected himself (the Hawaiians did not use contractions, and he tried to adjust his speech to conform) "let us see if we can find some common ground on which to start our discussion."

"I am sorry!" Takeo started to apologize for what seemed to her to be brash inconsideration on the part of the young women. If a minister were to lose face in her home at the hands of her guests, she would be mortified.

"Oh, do not be sorry!" Del smiled reassuringly as he sought to allay her fears, "I am going to enjoy this immensely!" Then, turning back to his questioners, he inquired, "Do you believe in science?"

"Oh, yes, we teach science in high school," Lora explained.

"All right, then, do you believe that you really exist . . . that you really are?"

"Yes-s-s," Leiko replied hesitantly. She did not intend to be tricked into any commitment that would compromise her position.

"Do not be afraid." He laughed good-naturedly at her caution. "I am not going to try to out-maneuver you. I just want to find somewhere we can start to answer your questions. If you really do exist, how did you come into being?"

Through a series of questions, counter-questions, illustrations, and exchange of ideas, the seventy and the teachers got back to the Intelligence that designed the universe. Del explained that he called that Intelligence "God." The girls agreed to the use of the term, and from that point they worked back to the discussion of God as creator, the testimony of the Scriptures of his nature, his mighty acts, and his relationship with man. Finally they came, after several encounters, to the revelation of God through his Son, Jesus Christ.

"I think you will understand him better," Del told them, "if you read of his life and ministry from the testimony of two nations." With that opening he introduced Leiko and Lora to the Book of Mormon, and they each took a copy to read.

It was soon after this that trouble arose in Leiko's family. Her twin sister, Reiko, had fallen in love with a young man of Chinese Hawaiian ancestry and announced her intention to marry him. Papasan Hashida held a place of high reputation in his community of fellow Japanese, and there were strong social rules for the behavior of his children. One of the rules said that the boys could, if it seemed necessary and advisable, marry "down" from their social position. The girls, however, must marry "up" or not at all. For one of them to marry a darkskinned and—from their point of view—less socially elite Chinese or Hawaiian was disgraceful and would mean loss of reputation for the family patriarch.

The problem was of such consequence that drastic measures were justified, it seemed to the family. Since Reiko would not "listen to reason," she must be stopped from perpetrating this reproach upon her family. For her father to have to discipline his errant daughter was likewise disgraceful. So, being the eldest loyal daughter, Leiko could see no way out except that she perform her duty, whatever it might cost her. She determined to execute her purpose for the honor of her father. When the troubled schoolteacher came to the mission house for her lesson she confided in us.

"Father says he will kill her!" The attractive young Japanese spoke with a ferocity that her slight body denied. "But he will not have to. I will kill her myself!" and she gritted her teeth as though preparing for the act.

We were horrified by the pronouncement.

"Why?" I asked, trying to maintain an outward calm. It was evident that the white-lipped girl meant every word she said. With a quick glance at Del, I continued, "She is your sister . . . your twin sister. Why must you kill her?"

"We will have another chance to get together before you go home, will we not?" Del made no effort to dissuade the determined young woman. "Perhaps you can read most of the Book of Mormon this week. Forget about the history involved. Do not be concerned if the story gets a little tangled; just concentrate on the testimony the book bears of the Christ."

We prayed frequently during the week for the troubled family so close to tragedy and for Leiko's understanding of the Master whom she was just learning to know.

"I will not have to kill Reiko after all," she announced happily when she returned to the mission house for her next lesson.

"Did Reiko change her mind?" Del asked.

"No." Leiko smiled and shook her head. "I changed my mind! As I read the Book of Mormon I came to see life a lot differently. There is no reason why Reiko should not marry the man she loves, even if he is darker than she and of another nationality."

"But what about your father?" Del needed to know that Leiko had thoroughly evaluated the situation.

"I am sure I can help him to see it my way." The young woman was confident. "I always have been able to influence him more than the others."

* * * * *

"We just returned from the wedding," Leiko's letter brought the good news. "All of the family attended, and Father gave Reiko and Rick his blessing. Now Peter and I are planning our wedding. We want to be married in August when you are in Oahu for the reunion. Will you please marry us then?"

"It's a long jump from murder to blessing," Del remarked after reading the letter aloud—and he didn't care that he had used a contraction. "Only the Lord could bridge it so smoothly!"

TAKING GOD AT HIS WORD

"I want to go to Graceland College," the young Nisei spoke earnestly.

"Fine, fine," Delbert responded. "Do you have your money all together?"

"I do not have any money," Ruth replied, "but you told me that I could have the thing I most desired in all the world if I continued to participate faithfully in the work of the Lord. I have done the best I can, and I want to go to Graceland."

"Well, let's see." Del was hesitant. "Maybe you will have to do as I did—take time out and work a year."

"But I want to go this year," the girl was emphatic, "and you promised."

"You are right." Del had promised . . . in the name of the Lord. It was at the Wednesday evening prayer service that preceded a series of meetings to be held by a visiting seventy. Del had felt the Spirit of God directing him to speak to Ruth and Peter, Stan and Don, but he had hesitated. Such a promise—the thing they wanted most! How could he give such a promise even for the Lord? The service closed, and he had not spoken. When the impress of the Spirit grew unmistakable, Del hurried to gather the four young people into the area adjoining the rostrum that was once the mission house living room but now doubled as classroom and lounge.

"I have a confession," he began. "The Lord wanted me to speak to you during the service, but I did not do it. Now I know I must. Since I failed to speak during the service I feel I must give you the message now. *If you will continue in your efforts to serve the Lord and to be diligent, particularly in the coming experience of this congregation, the promise of the Lord is to you that he will grant you the fondest desire of your hearts.*"

The Spirit of God engulfed the small group in testimony as he spoke, but even with such verification the promise seemed overwhelming.

"Will you please tell us again?" Ruth wanted to make sure that she had heard correctly.

Delbert repeated the message, and the little group disbanded, awed by the presence and promise of God.

Ruth had accepted the challenge of the Lord. Every night of the series found her at the church supporting the service. Each opportunity to serve found her cheerfully doing all she could. Now she was ready to claim the Lord's promise.

"You are right," Del agreed. "You do have the Lord's promise. With your faith you will go to Graceland this year."

Days later Ruth arrived at the state's capital city where job opportunities were far more prevalent than in her hometown.

"Oh, Ruth," the district president had greeted her. "I hear you are going to Graceland."

"That's right," Ruth responded happily.

"Do you have all your money?" he inquired.

"I do not have any of my money yet," she replied.

"Your parents will help you?" The district president could not believe that this young girl could really get all the money required to travel the 4,000 miles to Graceland College, purchase an entirely new wardrobe for the cold climate of Iowa, and pay for the year at school as well.

"My parents cannot help me at all," she said. "My father is old, and my brother has more than he can do to support his own family and help my folks. I will have to do it alone. But then I am going to work at two jobs this summer."

"You are? Where are you working?"

"Oh, I do not have a job yet, but I have applied for two," she said, explaining the prospects.

When she had finished, the district president shook his head wonderingly but with admiration. "Yes, Ruth, I believe that with your faith you *will* make it."

Summer had almost passed when we next saw Ruth. Her two jobs had kept her so busy that she barely had time to visit the reunion grounds the first weekend. She came especially to talk to Delbert.

"Brother Smith," she spoke seriously, "I do not know what to do. I still lack $400 of the money I must have to go to Graceland. If I am not going, I must write this week or lose my deposit. What shall I do?"

"What happened to your faith?" Del teased. She looked so serious that he couldn't resist a little kidding.

"I just do not know." She smiled momentarily, but this was a serious matter.

"Ruth, how did you get all but the $400?" Del was serious now too.

"Well, I applied for and got a work assignment and a loan at Graceland, and I have had these two jobs all summer." She had not quite understood the question.

"What ever made you believe in the first place that you might have a chance to go to Graceland this fall?" Del continued.

"You told me I could," Ruth was remembering, "but

maybe I did not do enough for the Lord. Maybe I was asking too much to go this year." Discouragement had almost convinced her of her unworthiness.

"You have come so far, Ruth; why give up now? I cannot tell you what to do, but I will ask the Lord to help you make the best possible decision."

Toward the end of the week Ruth returned for a second brief visit to the reunion grounds.

"What did you decide?" Del asked, though he thought he knew.

"I did not cancel," she said happily.

Reunion closed. We remained overnight awaiting a flight to our home the next morning. Late that night we were aroused by the telephone.

"Brother Smith." It was Ruth, and she was crying.

"What is the matter?" Delbert was solicitous and concerned. "Tell me what has happened."

There was a long pause while the girl struggled to control her voice. Finally it was out. When she had returned from work at 11:30 p.m., her second job, there was a message: "Father suffered heart attack. Cancel college plans. Return home immediately." The blow was just too much.

"Brother Smith," she sobbed, "what shall I do?"

"Don't do anything tonight," Del advised. "Get your sleep, and we'll both pray about it. Then in the morning we will talk about it again."

There was no call from Ruth in the morning. We went to the airport and prepared to depart. Suddenly a girl ran toward us calling, "Brother Smith!" Ruth was radiant.

"What is it?"

"I will not have to give up Graceland after all." The words tumbled over each other like rocks tumbling back toward the sea with the undertow.

"Tell us what happened!"

After Del had advised her to wait until morning to make a decision Ruth had gone to her shower. As she showered she prayed for direction. Over the noise of the water she heard a Voice saying, "Ruth, your father will be all right."

She listened. Was she imagining things? The Voice came again: "Your father will be all right."

"So they will not need me at home," Ruth concluded. "But how am I going to tell them?" Her parents were Buddhists and would not look with favor on her experience with a Voice.

"I do not know," Del answered honestly.

"I know I will have to go home to tell them," she continued.

"That will cost you an extra forty dollars," he reminded her.

"I know." Ruth was aware of the extra drain on her financial resources. "But I cannot make them understand by letter. I will have to go."

"In the meantime we will be praying for God's direction for you. Just keep up your faith," Del was reassuring.

On the day we reached home we found the mail stacked high. Among the letters awaiting us was a check for $385—for a debt my brother was repaying.

"Del," I called excitedly after having opened it, "here is Ruth's money."

"Good, good," he said, "but somehow I doubt that Ruth will need it."

On the street later that day Del met a friend, a former Gracelander. "Did Ruth get my letter?" Bud Scott inquired.

"Letter? If she did she didn't mention it."

"You know I have been working as a recreation director for the Settlement House this summer," Bud, whose profession was physical education and coaching, explained. "I found that there is a $400 scholarship available at the

Settlement that has not been taken this year. I am certain Ruth can get it."

"Wonderful!" Del was ecstatic.

"She had better apply soon," Bud continued.

"She will be home early next week," Del explained. "If she did not get your letter, we can tell her then."

The summer's work ended, Ruth returned to her home and called us.

"I am home," she announced, "and I have to tell my family that I am leaving again—this time for Graceland. There will be a gathering tonight. . . . How shall I tell them?"

"I still do not know," Del had to confess. "But we will be praying for direction for you. Incidentally did you get Charles Scott's letter?"

Briefly he explained about the available scholarship. "I will apply in the morning," Ruth promised.

* * * * *

"Brother Smith." The voice on the telephone was suffused with emotion.

"How did it go?" Del had waited and prayed for hours.

"Oh, Brother Smith," the emotion was joy, "for the first time in my life I felt really part of the family."

"How did you do it?"

"I do not know," Ruth asserted. "I only know that it came so naturally." She explained how her loved ones had gathered to greet her and how she had been able, through a power not her own, to explain to them all that had transpired.

"Now they want me to go to Graceland." Her joy could not be contained. "And they want you and Sister Smith to come to our home. Could you come now?"

"We will be there in a few minutes." Del's joy was matched by Ruth's.

Graciously her parents and brother greeted us when we arrived at the Usui home.

"We are grateful for all you church people have done for Ruth," they said. "We did not understand. But now that we do understand, we too will do all that we can to help her do this thing she wants so much to do."

Since her application for the Settlement scholarship could not be processed before she had to go to Lamoni I suggested, "Let us send our check to Graceland and ask that it be held for security until the scholarship money is available."

Soon there was a letter from Ruth. "Please give the Settlement board members my address," it read, "so that when the scholarship is approved they can send the money directly to me."

Del smiled broadly. "Notice," he said, "she doesn't say '*if*' the scholarship is approved, she says '*when.*' Thank God for faith like Ruth's!"

BONDS AROUND THE GLOBE

"John Kim Lim." The big voice of the Afro-Asian Conference leader boomed out the name over the airport's speakers. Hastily Delbert glanced at the paper in his hand. Yes, that was one of the men who was to spend the weekend at our home. He stood tiptoe to stretch his six feet to six feet two and looked over the crowd. It was easy to locate the tall young Chinese from Malaya who was to be our guest.

"Buddhist" the paper said.

"Abdullah Lebdah," announced the voice. That was the other . . . dark, curly-haired Abdullah from Jordan.

"Islam—no pork, no alcoholic beverages" the paper stated.

For weeks we had been looking forward to this day. The local branch of the university was hosting the Afro-Asian student conference sponsored by the U.S. State Department for the weekend, and the American Association of University Women—of which I was the local social studies chairman—was arranging housing for the members of the conference.

For a time it had appeared that we would not be fortunate enough to have any of the guests. Far more luxurious homes and more prominent people were available to host the students, and the committee felt that the guests should be housed with them. But the list of available homes grew shorter and shorter as the conference deadline drew near. One after another the prominent people canceled their invitations. Abdullah and John were finally assigned to us.

Del pushed through the crowd, identifying paper in hand, to greet the two young men, while I stood on the periphery of the intent group answering the flood of questions the little ones asked and lifting them in turn to see the two guests.

At the mission house dinner was already prepared. A snowy white cloth covered the folding picnic table set up in the living room for the occasion. Crystal goblets sparkling beside the melmac table setting apparently startled Abdullah, and he spoke quickly, fearing his request that no alcoholic beverages be served was not being honored.

"My faith is Islam," he declared with dignity. "I cannot drink alcoholic beverages."

I smiled at the thought of alcoholic beverages being served in our home.

"We know," I assured him. "Those are for water only. I do not even have coffee or tea for you, but . . ."

"What a relief!" he broke in gratefully. "I have never tasted such terrible coffee as has been served me here. And the tea is like bad water!"

"We do have milk," I continued, "and we have a cereal beverage. Would you like to try it?"

Both John and Abdullah requested it.

"This is good!" Abdullah voiced his surprise and delight when he tasted the drink. "I must know how this is made. I want to introduce this beverage to my country."

Dinner finished, Delbert broached the subject of itinerary with John and Abdullah. "There is a Zion's League meeting at the mission tonight," he told them. "Our young people would love to have you tell them of your countries, your religions, and your reason for being here." The guests exchanged glances. "Of course, if you have other plans..." he assured them.

"Oh, no!" protested the young men together. "We want to go to meet your group. That's why we are here," Abdullah explained. "It is just that two young ladies, students of the university here, have asked to take us around tonight, and we have agreed to go with them," added John.

"But we will just take them with us," Abdullah spoke confidently.

At League time, however, Abdullah and John entered the church alone in serious conversation.

"They are Catholic," John was explaining as they came toward us, "and they are forbidden to enter this sanctuary."

"But why?" Abdullah was not to be easily satisfied, and he turned his puzzled countenance almost accusingly toward Del. "Aren't you both Christian? Why can't the Catholics come to this church with us? I'm not even Christian, and you invited me."

Patiently Delbert explained that we would gladly welcome the girls regardless of their faith. Their religion—not ours—excluded them from entering. Abdullah was still puzzled, almost unbelieving, and he turned to John for some indication of his feeling on the matter. "Mr. Smith is right," John assured him. "It is their faith that excludes them, not ours."

"Not ours?" It was Del's turn to be puzzled. "The paper states that you are Buddhist. Are you not?"

"No," smiled John. "I am a Wesleyan. I follow the Christ too."

Del nodded understandingly. That was why John had seemed so much more at ease in our home than had Abdullah. Prayer time had found John comfortable while Abdullah was restless. Abdullah's fierce loyalty to his nation and its leaders—and his just as intense hatred of some other nationalities—had not been reflected by John. Rather his love of people and understanding of others seemed to transcend the boundaries of his native Malaya and to embrace all people—even the stormy Jordanian with whom he was visiting in our home.

The memorable weekend passed quickly. After what seemed only a few hours we were again at the airport. John and Abdullah were taking pictures and saying their good-byes.

"You'll write me all the information you can get about that beverage," Abdullah reminded me. "I really want to introduce that drink to my country. Why, if it's really made of grains we can produce it there."

"Of course I will," I promised.

The letter was written.

There was a thank-you message from Abdullah written in Arabic, a napkin ring, and a crucifix sent from Jerusalem. Abdullah just couldn't understand the division of Christianity that made the crucifix sacred to some and not to others. And each year at Christmas there was a letter from John and his growing family. Because of these friends we were welded by love and precious memories to to two more nations. To reach them our thoughts must circle the globe.

A BRAVE WOMAN

"Keala . . . Kalani, your mother was the bravest woman we ever knew! Dr. Mitchell wants you to know." Nancy Mitchell had driven to the mission house to bring Veda's nursing pin. "You will place it on her uniform, won't you?" she asked Del. "Veda wanted to be buried wearing it."

"What a woman!" he spoke his admiration fervently. "And she told us she was a coward!"

Just weeks before I had noticed the rapid distention of Veda's abdomen and the telltale change in the color of her skin. "Del," I had questioned, "have you noticed the change in Veda? I'm afraid she has cancer."

"Has she said anything to you?" he asked.

"Not a word, but you just notice the next time you see her."

It wasn't long until Veda came to the mission house to visit. Busy as she was as chief surgical nurse at Puuamaile Hospital she rarely had time for visiting. There were days off when she and I had climbed the mountain to pick luscious red thimble berries or had taken the children to the ocean to play on the rugged lava worn smooth by the constant washing of the waves. And there was always time for church. Veda's class was a favorite in the church school, and her contributions to the work of the women were invaluable.

Sometimes Charlie, her stately Hawaiian husband, could attend church with her and the children, but his work as a tour guide kept him on the road on many occasions when he would have liked being with his family. Charlie Warren was not *just* a tour guide; he was the dean of all the guides on the Big Island—a real Hawaiian who knew his people's history, legends, and language as no other guide knew them. Veda had met him on the ship when she first came to the Islands as a young nurse just graduated from the School of Nursing at the Independence Sanitarium and Hospital.

Keala and Kalani, the Warrens' two children, were best friends of our children. Kalani could spend hours with the boys exploring lava caves, building forts in the tall California grass, or just picking the guava that grew in the grove near the mission house. Steven loved to tease Keala in kindergarten and often tugged mischievously at her silky black braids.

"Have you noticed?" Veda asked, and she glanced at her protruding abdomen.

I nodded, not trusting myself to speak.

"All of a sudden I look as big as you," and she laughed a little as I glanced at my own enlarged figure. But mine was temporary. I knew, as I carried our fifth child, that mine was a productive protrusion.

"Do you know what has caused it?" It was a ridiculous question, I knew, but I did not dare voice my fears.

"It is cancer," Veda declared resolutely, though tears did fill her eyes. "Dr. Mitchell is trying everything he knows. Why, I'm even getting gold sloshed around in my insides!" and she laughed again.

"Did you want Delbert to administer to you?" I knew that Veda was more willing to give than to receive.

Veda nodded. "If he would," she said simply.

There were other administrations, and many prayers of

the Saints in Veda's behalf. Often after she taught her class and attended the morning service at the church she would be weary and ill. With the imposition of the elders' hands on her head and the ministry of the Spirit which they brought, the weariness would be lifted and the pain relieved, but healing did not come.

A bed was moved into her nursing station at the hospital. When the weariness and pain were too severe, Veda would lie down and rest awhile, then return to her place by the doctor's side.

When it became apparent that neither gold nor X ray nor any other known treatment would be effective, Delbert took a magazine on one of his visits. "Veda," he suggested, "I think you might like to read this." "This" was the *Reader's Digest* story titled, "My Last Best Year on Earth," written by a young wife and mother whom we had known back in Iowa who had met her confrontation with incurable cancer with amazing, unselfish courage.

* * * * *

"I will not be here to teach my class next Sunday," Veda had announced one Sunday. "I have always wanted to go to Kauai. Charlie is going to take me next weekend."

That same week Leila Miyamoto had accompanied her husband who had come to the Big Island to minister to the congregation there. Leila and Veda had been friends from their student nursing days. At the airport as she left Leila had instructed me, "Let me know when Veda is bedfast. I want to come back and care for her."

* * * * *

"Will you please come?" It was Charlie on the phone when the weekend was finished. "Veda wants you."

We hurried up the long hill road that led from the mission

house to the beautiful home of the Warrens. Veda had painted it herself during her vacation the past summer, and it stood fresh and inviting in its setting of lush tropical foliage.

Inside, too, the house spoke of meticulous housekeeping and loving care. The tasteful furnishings and flawless floors mirrored the warm personality of the gentle homemaker and the willing discipline of her family.

We stopped short as we entered the living room. Only careful discipline kept us from gasping in astonishment at the sight before us. On the divan Charlie sat, Veda's body gently cradled in his arms. But what a change eight days had made! Her flesh seemed to have melted away. The woman Charlie held was a fragile shadow of the Veda we had known. Her gaunt cheeks were accented by prominent cheekbones that had been previously obscured by soft flesh. Thin skin barely masked the starkness of the frontal bones across her forehead. Only her eyes seemed really alive, and they glowed softly out of deep socket wells to plead her cause.

"Pray for me, Delbert." Her voice was still strong and steady. "Pray for me once more. Only this time, do not pray that God will heal me. Just pray that it will be quick. I'm an awful coward!"

When we returned the following day, Veda was lying in her bed. "They wanted me to go to the hospital," she said, "but why should I leave my home and Charlie and the children? There is nothing more that anyone can do." Then with a bit of a sigh she relaxed on her pillow and began to talk of her anticipation for her future almost eagerly as though she were sharing her plans for an exciting and long-anticipated trip. "I wouldn't mind at all if it were not for Charlie and the children," she finished wistfully.

"There is still a chance," I wanted to be realistic but . . .

"No, Mildred." Veda's voice sounded a bit weary. "But it is going to be quick. That is my blessing."

Her long trip began the next day. "She just turned her face to the wall and died!" asserted the startled nurse who sat by her side. "I have never seen anything like it!"

"Yes, Keala and Kalani, your mother was a brave and wonderful woman," Del and I agreed.

WITH HANDS OF FAITH

"The child is not here. We released her this morning." It was the professional voice of the hospital receptionist who answered Delbert's request to visit the little girl in the isolation ward. Then forgetting her professional stoicism, she stared quizzically at the tall young man across the desk from her. "It was meningitis, was it not?"

"Yes, Dr. Mitchell said it was meningitis," Del returned, his voice trailing off in grateful reverie as he turned to leave the hospital. How thankful he was for the experience of yesterday! He could hear again the doctor's measured tone as he had counseled him.

"The decision will have to be yours, but I want you to know that there is grave danger for anyone who is near her."

"It is a contagious form of meningitis?" Del had asked.

"Yes," the doctor replied, "an extremely contagious form."

"Would there be danger to others if I should go in?"

"The infection can be carried to others. If you decide to go, you will have to be subject to all the precautions that the nurses and I follow in the isolation ward."

For a moment Del had hesitated as he had thought of his own small children at home. He could remember the horrible deaths suffered by those whom he had known in his youth who had been victims of the virulent menengococci—the ruptured eyeballs, the broken eardrums, the damaged brains. Still, he had been called to administer to this young girl who now tossed restlessly in her bed down the hall in the isolation ward, the terrible ache in her head and back beginning to dull from the medication, the persistent fever still raging unabated. He had gone directly to the isolation ward expecting to carry out his mission, but the nurse had stopped him with her authoritative, "You cannot go in there. She is quarantined."

"But I must go in," he had insisted. "I am a minister, and her parents have called for me."

So the nurse had taken him to the doctor whose efforts to dissuade him had momentarily weakened his resolution. Then it had happened. Deep inside his consciousness Delbert felt as well as heard the words: "Yea, though I walk through the valley of the shadow of death, I will fear no evil; for Thou art with me."

The decision had been made. Outfitted in surgeon's gown and mask, he had entered the little girl's room while her parents had waited anxiously on the screened walkway that skirted the area.

When the ordinance had been completed, Del had scrubbed and returned to his regular clothing. He had ministered with assurance to concerned parents, one of whom was a Catholic and unaccustomed to the faith of the Saints.

And now in less than a day—overnight, in fact—she was well . . . completely well . . . and at home with her family.

A happy smile crossed Del's face and his heart sang as his eyes swept upward beyond the banyan tree, across the snowcapped mountain into the clear blue tropical sky, and his lips moved in a silent prayer of gratitude. A tremor of joy passed through his body as he smartly snapped one closed fist into the open palm of the other hand in a characteristic gesture and strode with a gait that would have been a happy skip if he had been younger, down the flower bedecked hospital walk to his car.

CLARA AND THE BIG WAVE

"Clara is dead!" sobbed the young Nisei as she ran into my outstretched arms. "Did you hear? Clara is dead!"

"Clara?" I repeated the name dazedly. Surely not Clara. There must be some mistake. Clara was young and competent and faithful. Clara was needed. She was always getting others out of trouble. How could she be dead? "Are you sure?" I tried to comfort the girl as I looked toward the young Hawaiian-Japanese priesthood member who had accompanied her and the other girls to our house to share the sad news.

"The tidal wave," he said simply. "Clara and Etsuko were both killed."

"Oh, no!" I had seen on the neighbor's TV some of the devastation wrought by the tidal wave. I had watched only minutes, for as I saw the familiar signboards sticking out of the rubble on the almost unrecognizable streets and watched the people picking through it looking for family and possessions I had burst into tears and turned my back on the terrible scene. If only we had been there . . . maybe we could have helped! The mission house was high up on the mountainside. It would certainly have been untouched. We could at least have given shelter to some of the homeless.

But we were not there. In mid-March we had received word that we were to be moved from the Islands. "You can take your choice," the official letter had read. "You may come home for Conference or wait until school is out in June."

It had been a difficult choice to make. Plans were already made for a series of meetings to keep the people informed of the proceedings of the Conference. And there were so many things Delbert had hoped to do before he left the Islands! On the other hand we had already missed one Conference, and Del and the older boys had not been home in four years. I had returned to the mainland with baby Karen when my father had died two years earlier, but now there was baby Douglas whom none of the family had seen. There was a new prophet-president of the church and Del wanted a chance to be with him at work in the Conference.

If we left for Conference, however, the older boys would have to change schools, but there were some good things to be said for getting children acquainted with their new school friends before the summer holidays began. It would be difficult with only two weeks to go to get reservations for overseas shipment of possessions and transportation for the family. A great deal of money could be saved if we could get on the unscheduled flight with the others who were going to Conference from the Islands. Although we were loathe to leave so abruptly, it seemed best to go.

As soon as the decision was made, I called the wharf to see when we could get booking for our possessions. "Have them on the dock by five p.m. Thursday," the harbor master said, "all crated and ready for shipment."

I was stunned. This was Tuesday! How could we possibly

have them ready Thursday? For two days and nights Del worked taking little time out for sleep. Even then we had to call for a permit for late entry into the port area when it became apparent we could not quite make the five o'clock deadline. With the shipment made, however, it was simple to catch the unscheduled flight with the others. The Saints even had an Aloha party for us at the church. I thought I had never seen one so lovely or heard the Island songs sung more beautifully. I was filled with love and gratitude for the good people and could not half express my thanks. Delbert did better. His tears did not get in the way quite as much as mine did.

When the tidal wave struck in May, I had deep qualms about our decision to come to Conference. Maybe we had not prayed enough about it ... it had happened so fast. Maybe the Lord still needed us in the Islands.

Then the young Hawaiians who were attending Graceland College began to call us at our home in Lamoni, our new assignment. Carole and Mieko's homes were in the Waikea Kai area which had been devastated by the wave. Judy's father had a fishing fleet anchored in the harbor. Stanley lived at the edge of Reed's Bay which would certainly have felt the full force of the destructive melee. There was no way to know what had happened to any of their families, their possessions, or their friends. We had gathered the young ones together and waited with them, praying for their homes and loved ones, comforting and assuring them the best we could.

Now word had come that Clara and Etsuko were dead. Etsuko was loved by them all, but it was Clara who had taken the lead in helping to establish the mission church in Waikea Kai where they had heard the gospel. It was she who had talked to most of their Buddhist parents and obtained permission for their baptisms. It was she who had taught them in church school, cooked for them at youth camp, paid their way, helped them to develop their talents, encouraged them to go to college.

"Do you know how it happened?" Delbert questioned.

"They were at the Ululani Street Church when the first warning came," Stanley began.

"They were safe there," I interrupted. "No wave could reach that high."

"That is just it. They went back into the threatened area to get Etsuko's parents. Mrs. Yamamoto went to the car willingly, but Etsuko's father refused to leave. You know how precious his orchids were to him." We nodded.

"He declared no wave had ever touched their home before and this one would not come near either. He was not about to leave all that he had worked so hard for during his life," Stanley continued. "And he did not. He went with it, and so did Etsuko and Clara."

"And Mrs. Yamamoto?" Delbert inquired.

"She was still waiting in the car when the wave hit. Remember Clara's little Volkswagen? The wave made a boat of it and carried Mrs. Yamamoto to safety. They found her sitting in the car seven blocks *Mauka* (toward the mountain) from where their home had been."

"Have they found Clara and Etsuko?" I knew that it took a long time to find bodies in rubble left by tidal waves, and often those that were washed out to sea were never found.

"They found Clara terribly hurt but still alive over by Nora Nobeta's house." We pictured the spot just across the road from the little Quonset church that housed the mission Clara and Etsuko had given so much to establish. "She died in the hospital later. The word came at Clara's funeral that they had found Etsuko's body. They have not found Mr. Yamamoto. Apparently he was washed out to sea."

"Buy why Clara?" The girls were calmer now and could talk about the tragedy. "We needed her so. What will the mission do without her?" Each of the young folk had family and friends still worshiping in the Quonset.

"I do not know why Clara," Del replied. "Maybe some of the others will get busy now and assume the responsibilities they should have been carrying for a long time. But I can see how God ministered to her needs before her death. Do you know why Clara had a Volkswagen," Delbert asked, "instead of the beautiful red and black Plymouth she used to keep so meticulously? One could have eaten right off the floor of it."

"I remember the Plymouth all right." Stanley, whose own family could not afford a car, had admired the Plymouth too often not to remember it. "I always wondered why she sold it."

"You remember when Brother Tsunao Miyamoto was on the Big Island to minister to us?" Del was certain they would recall the visit of the venerable bishop's agent. "Remember the night he came? We had an Aloha for him at the Ululani Street Church, and he told us why he had come. I'll never forget the kind look on his face as he said it. 'I did not come here to scold you folk,' he assured us. 'I just came to save you from the burning.' Remember how he quoted the scripture passage, 'He that is tithed shall not be burned,' and cautioned us to heed the warning, 'If any man shall take of the abundance which I have made, and impart not his portion according to the law of my gospel, unto the poor and the needy, he shall, with the wicked, lift up his eyes in hell, being in torment.' I was impressed that he said it so lovingly and did not even need to have a Doctrine and Covenants in his hand to quote it. It was truly his message from God to us!

"Clara felt it, too," Del continued, "and believed that Brother Miyamoto was speaking for the Lord. She owed quite a bit of tithing and then and there determined to pay it. So she sold her beautiful Plymouth and bought the Volkswagen so she could save money to pay her tithing.

"When income tax time came, Clara usually just signed the short form and took the standard deductions for contributions to charitable organizations. But this time the church treasurer reminded her of the large amount she had contributed to the church during the year and asked her to let him figure the long form for her so she could get a refund. You know that Jerry is a certified accountant as well as mission treasurer?" Del inquired.

As the young people nodded assent, he continued his narration. "Clara gave Jerry the information that he needed, and when he finished figuring, Clara got a refund of one hundred and twenty dollars. Interestingly, she still owed just one hundred and twenty dollars tithing. So she immediately set aside the refund to finish paying off her debt to the Lord.

"I wonder," Del finished reflectively, "if Clara did not look back many times and rejoice that she took Brother Miyamoto's ministry seriously." Than rallying from his reverie, he smiled at the rapt young Hawaiians, "God's love is unfathomable, is it not?" The students returned his smile through their tears.

Looking on, I thought that just maybe this was where God wanted my husband when the big wave hit.

RON MEETS DANIEL

"Mamma, was there a real Daniel?" our second son asked as I paused, resting my hands on the rim of the pan of bread dough I had been kneading when the telephone call had come. Mary Bixford had been on the phone. Her son and Ron were in the same church school class, and Mary had called to see if Ron had said anything about what they had been taught about Daniel the preceding Sunday. Something he had heard from my end of the conversation must have caused him to question now.

"Why do you ask?" I inquired.

"Our teacher said there wasn't a real Daniel," he explained. "She says one time years after he was supposed to have lived the Hebrew people were having bad troubles so some of their writers invented a hero they called 'Daniel' to encourage the people. Is that right?"

"What do you think?" I resumed kneading the dough, rolling and pressing it, feeling it grow pliable and elastic under my fingers.

"When we read the story last week on the way to Grandmother's I thought he sounded real." Delbert had always taken us with him when he went to minister if it was at all possible. Since some of the trips were fairly long we had learned to fill the time singing, playing games, or reading. I smiled as I recalled the Sunday morning not long before when we had arrived at our destination only to have the children chorus, "Let's go back and start over so we can read some more." We had been reading *The Quiet Miracle* that day. But just the week before Ron's questioning we had read the Book of Daniel from the Bible as we traveled to Grandmother's home for a visit.

"You get the Bible while I clean my hands," I instructed, "and let's see what we can find out. And, Ron," I called after him as he headed for his father's study, "we'll need the concordance too. Get the big one by Young, will you, please?"

Soon we were deeply engrossed in the study of the Scriptures. "Here it says that Daniel wrote his own dream." Ronald had found the seventh chapter of the book.

"Here it says, 'I Daniel had seen a vision.' "

"Here's one that says, 'I Daniel fainted.' " Ron giggled at the thought.

"Here's one that says, 'I Daniel understood.' "

"I found one that says, 'I Daniel was mourning.' " We checked reference after reference as Daniel spoke of the events of his life in first person.

"Well, it looks as if Daniel thought he was a real person," Ron exclaimed as he straightened up from the book.

"That could be a storyteller's way of relating a story, though," I reminded him. "Do you suppose anyone else who lived about the time he is supposed to have lived spoke of him? That might be more conclusive evidence that he really did live. At least it would tell us whether he was invented hundreds of years later."

"How can we find out?" Ron was anxious to know. This was a new idea to me, too, and I didn't know how the search would turn out. "Let's check the concordance," I suggested.

"It looks as if the name Daniel was used a lot of times." Ron had found the list.

"Are any of them the Daniel we are looking for?" I started checking. "This concordance really is helpful the way it identifies people. It says the Daniel spoken of by Ezekiel, the prophet, is the same Daniel referred to in the Book of Daniel."

"When did Ezekiel live?" Ron was thinking clearly.

"Well, he had one of his visions in the fifth year of King Jehoiachin's captivity, and Daniel went into captivity in the third year of the reign of Jehoiakim."

"How does that help?" Ron was getting confused.

"Doesn't it give some dates there?" He was hovering over the concordance. "If it doesn't we'll have to get the *Bible Dictionary*."

"Oh, here it says that Daniel was taken into Babylon in 604 B.C., and his last prophecy was given in 530 B.C."

"And Ezekiel started prophesying in the fifth year of Jehoiachin, which this author puts at 595 B.C. That would be just nine years after Daniel went into Babylon."

"Hey! Did you know that Jehoiachin was the son and successor of Jehoiakim?" Ron was excited. "That means Ezekiel and Daniel must have lived at the same time. What was it Ezekiel said about Daniel?"

"In the fourteenth chapter he classes him along with Noah and Job as righteous men. In the twenty-eighth chapter he speaks of him as a wise man who must have been known even to the prince of Tyrus."

"How about Jesus?" Ronald had another inspiration. "Did he ever mention Daniel?"

I consulted the concordance. "See what it says in Matthew 24:15, and I'll look at Mark 13:14. Oh, you have the Inspired Version of the Bible there; it will be the twelfth verse in it."

"It says he was a prophet whose prophecies they could expect to see fulfilled." Ron was still reading.

"Who was speaking?" I wanted to be sure.

"Jesus. He was telling his disciples what to expect before he returned to the earth."

"Mark must have been reporting the same event," I confirmed from my reading.

"Wow!" Ron was convinced. "If Daniel thought he was a real man, and Ezekiel thought he was a real man, and Jesus thought he was a real man, then I guess I won't worry about it!" And like a flash he was off to play.

"Sadie," I called my good friend and Ronald's teacher, "may Delbert and I come down to talk to you?"

"Come ahead," was the cordial reply.

We discussed with Ron's teacher the results of our study with Ron and the questions that initiated it.

"It is good to know he was challenged to study," was the teacher's sincere response.

A MESSAGE FOR THE WOMEN

The low hum of the sewing machine filled the room as the racing needle paced my thoughts. Karen's dress must be finished. The baskets of ironing and mending must be emptied. There were scores of things to be done to prepare a family of seven for reunion! And the garden! The tomatoes could be held over until after reunion if there could be enough refrigerator space located, but the corn and beans would have to be canned or frozen next week. How could I manage it all?

Suddenly other thoughts came crowding into my mind—startling thoughts, but every one bearing the imprint of truth. I had long since learned to recognize the movement of the

Spirit of God in my life and in my mind. Strange, though, was the knowledge that came with the thoughts that these were ideas that I should share with the women of the stake at the coming reunion. But how could this be? No one had asked me to teach or speak at the reunion, and the program had long since been planned. Even now Delbert was attending a staff meeting completing last-minute details to insure effective ministry for the week.

But the thoughts raced on—each one indelibly etching itself on my mind—and my entire body responded to the power with which they came. I felt warm and light as though some indistinguishable breeze had lifted me from my chair, caressed my body, and poured a vial of warm oil inside my breast. My hands trembled so that I could no longer hold the material for the dress straight before the needle. At the sound of Del's footsteps, I decided to check and see if any change of plans would require my help as an instructor at reunion.

"Who is teaching the women at camp?" I queried as he stepped through the doorway.

"Why, Sister Bellingham," Del looked puzzled. "You knew she was coming, didn't you?"

"Yes," I replied weakly, "I knew."

Without explanation, either of my question or of my haste, I hurried to the basement. If I could no longer sew, I could at least fold down the laundry. There was no time to spare even if I did need time to think.

As I stooped to remove the clothes from the drier, again there came a flood of thoughts reinforcing those that had come at the sewing machine. Again there came the instruction that these things were to be taught to the women at reunion. And again there came the physical response of my whole body to the power by which they came. The clothes dropped from trembling hands, and I thoughtfully ascended the stairs.

"Del, was anything said at the staff meeting about my speaking at the reunion?" I inquired.

"Not a word," he assured me. "Now, tell me, what's this all about?"

"I'm not certain... but I just had the strangest thing happen to me."

In meticulous detail I explained what had occurred in the sewing room and in the laundry. "I know every idea is valid," I finished, "but I would not dare say those things to the women unless God specifically commanded it. Besides, I'm not scheduled to speak! What do you make of it?"

"Just wait," Delbert spoke confidently. "If this is truly of the Lord—and I believe it is—you'll have your chance to speak."

The day passed rapidly, and by nightfall the events of the morning had been pushed to the back of my mind. When the phone rang, one of the children answered it.

"Mom," Alan called, "you're wanted on the phone."

"Mildred," it was the stake women's leader speaking, "on Thursday of reunion week we are going to have a special women's afternoon event. We would like for you to speak to us, if you will. You may use any topic you like. Can you do that for us?"

"I would be glad to do it," my response was immediate, but my voice trailed away in awe.

"Is something wrong?" Sister Campbell questioned with concern.

"Oh, no, nothing is wrong at all. After the meeting I'll tell you about it."

As Thursday drew near, I became increasingly concerned. I knew that my contribution to the meeting would not evoke gaiety. The ideas I had been directed to present would not be popular among a large segment of the group. In fact, they might even be interpreted as chiding, and that would not be helpful unless they were accepted with grace and spiritual perception.

"Oh, God, how can I do it?" I prayed as I reviewed my notes. "Wrongly taken, a talk like this could do irreparable damage to Del's ministry. How can I take the chance?"

As I prayed, my mind was impressed with the need to open the Book of Mormon. As I did, my eyes rested on the words of Lehi as he tried to explain to his older sons the behavior of their younger brother Nephi.

> Ye say that he hath been angry with you. But behold, his sharpness was the sharpness of the power of the word of God, which was in him; and that which ye call anger, was the truth, according to that which is in God, which he could not restrain. . . . Behold it was not him, but it was the Spirit of the Lord, which was in him which opened his mouth to utterance, that he could not shut it.

I read the scripture three times, then, placing the reference on my notes, I slowly closed the book. For a long while I sat meditating. Finally with resolution I prayed, "Lord, if you say, 'Do it,' I will do it and trust you to see that it is understood."

All day Thursday I fasted, and Del fasted with me, knowing full well the import of that afternoon women's meeting in the life of the congregation. We prayed that the same Spirit that had taught me would teach the women I would address.

When the time came for me to speak, I stood on stage at the front of the large assembly hall trembling, but not from fear. During the opening of the service I had looked from one familiar face to another and had felt my heart swell with love for these wonderful people who bore so much responsibility for the coming kingdom. That many were confused and unsure of themselves I was painfully aware. That some were rebellious was equally apparent. That God wanted to allay their fears and direct their lives in the moments to follow I was certain. If only I could be a worthy instrument in his hands! And now I stood trembling with the same power that had first instructed me to speak to their needs.

I spoke with assurance and love of the little things that destroy or build the kingdom. Again thoughts paced through my mind with order and clarity that I had long ago learned to identify as the influence of God's Holy Spirit. The ideas that had come so clearly and with such power were now fleshed out by illustrations taken from experiences with which the women were familiar. The women listened intently and appreciatively.

"What, then, should we do that these little things will not destroy us or impede the coming kingdom?" I questioned as I neared the close of my talk. "Just one thing is needful. And that one thing is made graphically apparent to us every time we kneel in communion with the Christ and his people and prepare to partake of the sacrament of the bread and wine. We do it that we may always *remember him,* that we may have *his* Spirit to be with us every moment of our lives."

With the service concluded, Sister Campbell and I walked backstage together. "That was just what we needed," the women's leader said through tear-brimmed eyes. "Why did you act so strangely when I asked you to speak?"

My heart singing with happiness, I told of how the message came to me as I sewed and laundered, and of how I had come to deliver God's message to the women with fear and trembling only to have God turn that experience into a moment of joy.

THE SEVENTY IN POLITICS

City elections were over, and a number of men had lost their seats on the city council. Some were angry, and Delbert was being blamed.

"I would like to have a statement from you," he had told each candidate for office, "to be published so the voters will know how you feel about the cost of a beer license in this town."

"Now, Delbert," Lew York countered, "you know the law. We have to issue a license to any qualified applicant. Joe is a good fellow. He runs a clean place. We couldn't afford to let him leave town."

"You mean Joe was about to close the beer parlor?" Del had learned first from the local paper's report of the council meeting that the cost of a beer license in the city had been substantially reduced by the council, but he had not known that there was a possibility that the establishment would be closed if the old rates were maintained.

"Well," the councilman replied defensively, "he said the tax was too high and he would have to quit if we did not lower it."

"So you lowered it? Would it be so bad if our community did not have to support such an institution?" Del knew something of the way the people of the city felt. He had just joined the ministerial alliance of the area to alert the people of the entire county to their opportunity to prohibit the institution of hard liquor by the drink in their communities, even though new legislation permitted it in the state in any county that did not specifically prohibit it. When the final vote was taken, the Saints of our city were credited with the victory. His conviction that he was right to enter the political arena in this situation was growing with every revelation of fact surrounding the lowering of the tax.

"We just couldn't see our town without a beer parlor," asserted Lew. "Why the economy here is so marginal that if we lost the business of five farmers because they could not get beer locally, we could go bankrupt! Besides, if he were to leave town, there's no telling what sort of person might be next to apply for a license."

"The council has the right to close a business if the owner violates the law, doesn't it?" Del was serious about the matter. "What of our young people? We are a predominately Reorganized Latter Day Saint community here, and we have the youth of a large part of the church outside our town to consider."

"Oh, but you can't legislate righteousness!" came the quick reply.

Del smiled ruefully and shook his head at the old cliché. Just that week the daily paper our sons delivered throughout a large part of the community had an editorial on the subject highlighted by a cartoon showing Moses returning from his encounter with the Lord in the holy mountain carrying the tablets of the law and the people objecting furiously, shouting, "You can't legislate righteousness!"

Del had heard, too, from some of Lew's students, how his effort to inform the community of the stand of the candidates on this issue had been derided in a class discussion of his objection to the reduction of the license fee. "Mr. York is right," one of the students had declared. "You can't legislate righteousness!"

"Of course you can't!" Delbert agreed with the student and now with the professor. "But you have studied the behavior of communities as I have, and you know there are well established sociological and scriptural observations that the development of righteousness can be substantially influenced by the legislated standards held by the community. If we are ever to establish Zionic communities we must have some sort of standards. I feel that it is my responsibility to participate in local political activities to help establish standards commensurate with the gospel we declare."

The student was quick to respond affirmatively to this reasoning. "It's good to see things in perspective," he observed at the close of the discussion. Lew was less tractable.

"Mildred tells me that when she brought the subject up in PTA meeting," Del continued, "and asked that it be referred to the legislative committee for study, one of the teachers commented that the kind of thinking the council had shown would indicate that a brothel could also be established in the community without interference from council."

"Really," Lew replied, "if someone wanted to open a brothel here, we couldn't stop it."

"But we ought to be able to!" Delbert affirmed.

From his interview with the councilman, my husband went to the Women's Christian Temperance Union with a proposal. "I am interviewing the candidates for election to the city council. Would you like to print their answers so all of the voters may choose intelligently whom they wish to direct the affairs of this city?"

And so it was done. The council was substantially changed, and there was anger—not just about the election but because a seventy was actively rejecting some of the ideas that were being introduced to the youth of the community by some of those who were replaced and their associates.

"Prof says your trouble is that you have not learned how to love," a group of students reported one Saturday afternoon when they had gathered at our home to talk. "If you really loved, you would let others think and teach as they pleased."

"Bob," Del addressed one of the students, "if I saw Jim," he indicated another, "put poison in a jug of milk and take a drink of it thinking it was vitamins, would I be showing my love by sitting quietly by and letting him pass the poisoned milk out to you and your friends?"

"Wel-l-l," Bob screwed up his face in mock horror as he looked at the glass of milk he had been drinking as accompaniment for the big sugary donut on his plate, "I'd have my doubts!"

"As I see it," Del continued, "I have a responsibility to try to get Jim to a doctor!" and he slapped Jim's knee companionably to emphasize the extent of his concern.

"Maybe my husband doesn't know how to love," I broke into the conversation, "but you'll never know the hours we have spent researching the ideas we find unacceptable and discussing our findings with those who teach them, or the days we have spent fasting and praying that neither they nor we will be misled irrevocably. Love may be a lot of things, but it isn't necessarily laissez faire at election time—or any other!"

THE SUBSTITUTE SERMON

Del had made careful preparation for this Sunday evening sermon. Previous experiences had taught him the high standards of ministry the Creston congregation was accustomed to receive. The unusual devotion of young and old alike challenged all ministers who served the group to do their best. It was his best that Delbert had sought prayerfully to offer.

Now he knelt beside the pastor's desk in the second floor study and prayed earnestly. "Dear heavenly Father, if you don't want me to preach the sermon I have prepared for tonight, what do you want me to preach?"

During the prayer service that preceded the sermon Del discovered that his best was not an adequate offering for this night. It was the custom of the congregation to gather at the church, fasting, an hour and a half before each Sunday evening meeting. From five o'clock until six they prayed for the minister, for those whom they had invited to the service with whom they hoped to share the gospel, and for the presence and ministry of God's Spirit in all that would be done in his name. When the prayers were ended, the people disbursed, going to pick up those for whom they had prayed, to reassemble for the preaching at six thirty.

As he listened to the sincere prayers of the Saints, Delbert became aware that the message he had prepared for the evening was not what would most adequately minister to their needs. God had something else in mind for that night. When the people went to pick up their friends, he quickly ascended the stairs to the pastor's study to talk the matter over with the Lord.

As he prayed, a passage of scripture from the Book of Mormon was impressed upon his mind. Rising quickly from his knees, he found the text and read it. No revelation burst upon his consciousness. No new ideas or brilliant interpretations flooded his mind. In fact, he didn't have a clue as to what he could or should say about that passage or the ideas it presented to bring ministry to the congregation already assembling below him. He was familiar with the inspiration of the Spirit and knew without a doubt that the Book of Mormon quotation was the scripture that he should read. Thinking that the setting for the passage might yield some enlightenment, he read that which went before, but even this did not help. Carefully he perused that which followed. Still there was no elaboration. Only the unmistakable assurance persisted that this scripture held the key to the message of the Lord for this people this night, obscure though that message remained to him. He read it again and again until it was fixed firmly in his memory.

There was a knock on the study door, and Paul Winans spoke. "It's time to go into the service, Delbert,"

"Coming!" Del replied, closing his Book of Mormon slowly, still wondering what he would say when he faced the expectant congregation.

My husband loved the hymns of the church and was accustomed to singing them lustily when there was opportunity. During the opening of the service this evening, however, the sound of his voice was missing. Instead he continued talking to the Lord about the problem at hand.

"Father, what do you want me to say?" he pleaded. "If you don't give me something to say, I'll just have to read the scripture you've offered me and turn the preaching over to some of the other elders while I sit down. I know you've instructed us not to preach unless we have the Spirit," he continued, "and my mind is a total blank!"

The singing ceased. Vaguely Del heard Paul introducing him as the speaker of the evening and asking the members to uphold him in prayer. If only they knew! Del thought as he smiled a little wryly. He sat a moment with bowed head before he rose to take his place behind the podium. "I'll read the scripture, Lord," he prayed silently. "The rest is up to you."

Planting his feet firmly behind the pulpit to still the trembling of his body, he opened the Book of Mormon and read the passage now so clearly established in his consciousness. I always could tell whether my husband's sermons were inspired of God by the way he read his opening scripture. Tonight his voice was rich and full as he repeated the words of the ancient prophets. It reminded me of another time at a reunion when, inspired by the Spirit of God, he had read the scriptures assigned to him so beautifully that High Priest Wilbur Chandler had hurried to him at the close of the service, embraced him tearfully, and exclaimed, "Delbert, *nobody* can read like that!"

When he was finished, the congregation sang another hymn, but Del continued his prayer. "God, if you want someone else to bring the message this evening, I'd be grateful if you'd let me know who so I can designate my replacement."

During the hymn a few ideas dawned in his mind. "I'll present these thoughts," he resolved, "then I'll just tell the folk I don't have the Spirit of preaching tonight and I'll turn the pulpit over to whomever the Lord will indicate."

Having made this decision, he felt a calm spread over his body. As he arose again and approached the pulpit he hesitated only a moment. During that moment he became conscious of a person standing behind and a little to the right of him. "Good!" he said silently, "Paul is going to preach for me. He's just waiting for me to finish."

Then ideas began to rush into his mind. With fluency he rarely experienced he verbalized the ideas. While one portion of his mind comprehended and directed the verbalization, another continued to pray, "Lord, I'm totally dependent on you. I'll say what you give me to say, then I'll have to sit down." Again he felt the presence behind him and fleetingly wondered why Paul, or whoever it was, was still standing. After that he became so engrossed in the message he was delivering for the Lord that he forgot to wonder who it was or why. As one train of thought was exhausted, another flowed into his mind. The sermon lasted nearly an hour.

"That was the most beautiful sermon we ever heard you preach!" "Your sermon really ministered to me!" "Thank you, Brother Smith! That was an answer to my prayer!" The hushed reverence and tearful thanks of the people as they left the sanctuary testified of the ministry they had received.

"Brother Smith," Elder Dave Blair approached him when the congregation dispersed, "you had an unusual experience tonight, didn't you?"

"I surely did!" Del agreed.

"I think I saw something you didn't," the older man continued, his face glowing with wonder. "There was a personage standing just behind you and to your right."

"I know," Delbert confirmed David's testimony. "I felt him there, but I never did turn to see him."

"When you seemed to have finished what you had to say," David proceeded to explain, "he would lean toward you, and it seemed that he whispered. Then you would speak again with conviction and power!"

"A messenger sent from God!" Del said, awed.

"God has many ways of keeping his promise to be with us—even to the end of the world, doesn't he?"

THEORIES, FACTS, AND FAITH

"I want you seventies to know," the newly appointed biology instructor spoke emphatically, "that I am going to teach the students at this college evolution no matter what you say!"

Delbert and Ross Partridge looked quizzically at each other, and neither could resist smiling. They had no intention of telling their old friend what he should or should not teach. Besides Ross was not and never had been a seventy. They had come only to reminisce with Dale Darrington about old times—their own college days together.

"That's fine with me," Del responded amiably, "provided you teach it as a theory and not as a fact."

"It certainly is an accepted theory." Dale was a bit more at ease. Already this conversation had the makings of one of their old bull sessions, and the memory was pleasant.

"By all the men in your profession?" Del questioned.

"Well . . . not all." Dale was honest.

"But it is a theory," Del persisted, "not a completely proven fact."

"There are some missing data," Dale agreed.

"You know," Delbert leaned back in his chair with that prepare-for-a-lecture-look in his eye, "I had a tremendous professor at Montana School of Mines who gave me a worthwhile clue about the distinction between theory and fact, and I've found his advice to be sound."

"Go ahead." Dale and Ross both knew there would be no stopping him now.

"It was in geology class. Professor Antron was not only a great teacher but also a great geologist who was retained by Anaconda Mines at a high fee to help them locate veins of minerals, thereby saving them wasteful exploratory drilling. He was also president of the college. When he met our first class, he told us that the nature of the course was such that some might tend to lose their faith during it. 'But you do not need to lose your faith,' he declared, 'if you just remember one thing. Always distinguish between theory and fact. In science there are many theories, and they often conflict with each other. In religion, too, there are many theories which conflict. In both science and religion there are some facts. The facts of science and the facts of religion do not conflict. Theories may be based on a set of facts, but a set of facts does not guarantee that the resultant theory is factual. If you can keep clear in your mind that which is theory and that which is fact, you need not lose your faith.'

"You know," Del continued and the front legs of the chair hit the floor with a thump as he leaned forward, "the years have verified for me the validity of his teaching."

When Delbert and Ross returned to our home, they were still discussing Dale's brusque assertion of his intention to teach evolution. The conversation was disconcerting to me because Dale was my friend too. I was also concerned about the youth of the church who would be his students. If even one lost his way in the milieu it would be a tragedy. How should one react to the theories of evolution, anyway? There were many facts that the theories attempted to explain, but there were weaknesses in the explanations too. How *did* God create the earth and its inhabitants?

My mind raced again and again over what I had learned in my college classes, the ideas that had been propounded. I recalled the scriptural account of the creation, and as I thought I prayed, "Lord, help me to know."

In a flash my mind was directed to a favorite passage from Doctrine and Covenants 59. Quickly I turned to it and read, "And in nothing doth man offend God, or against none is his wrath kindled, save those who confess not his hand in all things, and obey not his commandments."

So that is it. None of our efforts to explain creation are offensive to God if we allow him his rightful place in the explanation. I smiled a little as I pictured God being amused at all our human efforts to explain how it had been done. I was sort of reminded of the way I tousled my own young son's blond curls and lovingly encouraged him to keep trying when he offered a baby solution for that which he could not yet comprehend.

LORI'S MISSIONARY FUNERAL

"Lori's dead," Olen said when Delbert took the long distance telephone call. "We want you to preach a missionary sermon at her funeral. She has been such a blessing to us while she has lived, we want her to be a blessing to others even in death."

"Of course, I will," Del agreed. "When is the funeral, and where?"

"We want to take her home to Illinois for burial," Olen explained. "There are so many people there with whom we want to share the hope of the gospel. Would Thursday be all right?"

"Thursday's fine," my husband answered. "Are you

going to send a funeral coach from Des Moines with the body?"

"No," Olen responded, "we thought we'd take her with us in the car."

"Would you like for us to take her?" Del suggested, realizing the added pain such a long journey would bring to the Henson family.

"Would you?" Relief and gratitude registered in the father's voice. "Linda and Donnie have felt a little strange about having the casket in the car."

"We'll be right up. When will Lori be ready for us?"

"We thought we'd leave tomorrow. Maybe, if you could come in the morning..."

Some two years before, while we were in Hawaii, we had shared Olen and Alice's surprise and joy at news that a baby was on its way. They had told us of their consternation when the child was born a mongoloid.

"She cannot live long," the doctor had explained, "... not with her weak heart. Just enjoy her while you can."

"But why?" Alice was grief stricken, "Why would we have a mongoloid child when the other two have been so perfect?"

"Nobody knows why," the doctor said gently. "It happens most frequently in older mothers, but nobody knows why for sure. You must not blame yourselves. Just enjoy her as long as she is with you."

Lori's body grew very slowly because of her inadequate heart, but her personality blossomed quickly—a result of all the love lavished upon her, the doctor said.

"Only such a sweet spirit could be housed in such a fragile body," Olen used to say as he played with the tiny, responsive youngster.

"Maybe the Lord might perform a miracle one day and give her a body to match her spirit," someone suggested once when we were visiting. But no one of them ever really dared to ask Him to do it.

World Conference was in the offing. The Hensons had been away in the Islands for several Conferences. Olen wanted to attend this one, and he wanted Alice and his teen-age children to be with him.

"Go," the doctor had urged Alice. "You need the change."

"But Lori?" Alice had questioned.

"Lori will be fine," the doctor assured her. "I know just the place for her to stay while you are gone," and he recommended a service operated by a group of Catholic nuns who were professionals in the care of young children.

Olen's careful investigation verified the doctor's recommendation, and for the first time in her young life Lori was left in the care of those outside the family.

When the Conference was finished the Hensons went directly to pick Lori up, intending that the whole family should arrive at home together.

"Just a moment," the receptionist said. "Let me call Sister Donahue."

The family waited happily anticipating their reunion with their blithe spirit.

"I'm sorry." Sister Donahue looked very grave. "Lori is dead. She passed away about an hour ago. We have been trying to get in touch with you."

"We were on the road on our way home," Olen explained as he drew Alice close to him as if to shield her from the blows he knew were falling on her heart. "What happened?"

"She just stopped breathing," the good sister explained. "The doctor said her heart just wore out."

"I'm glad in a way that it happened like this," Olen told us when we arrived with our own young ones to complete funeral arrangements and get Lori's body. "We knew it was coming, and this way Alice did not have to face it alone. I have prayed so often that Alice would not be alone when Lori died!"

Eyes closed, and dressed in a dainty baby dress that was still adequate for her even after more than a year and a half of life, Lori looked like a big doll nestled in the satin of the tiny casket. "We won't open it again," Olen announced firmly as they closed the lid to place it in the back seat of our car. "Down home we don't want people concerned about how she looks. We want them to know the love that gave her to us and now gives us hope for the future—even Lori's future. Make it a good missionary sermon, Delbert. Getting the people together to hear it will be Lori's last ministry on earth."

"May I leave the baby with you?" Del inquired of Jed Stewart who had just opened a funeral home in the bustling South Iowa town to which my husband was now appointed. "Somehow it doesn't seem quite right to leave her in the car or even to bring her into the house overnight."

Jed agreed and graciously took charge of the little body.

The long trip to Illinois began early Thursday and ended at the funeral home where the Hensons waited. The service followed at the church. The congregation Lori had called together was large and responsive, and the God, into whose presence she had returned, graced the meeting with his Spirit. In this setting, Del preached a meaningful missionary sermon for Lori.

A YOUNG MAN OF PROMISE

A mass of happy teen-agers piled out of their cars in front of our home one beautiful fall day. They were followed by their less exuberant adult drivers and sponsors. It was a field day for the Leaguers. They had traveled more than three hundred miles to visit Graceland College and had been overnight guests of the college on campus. Now, before their return home, they had stopped to greet us because we had once been in their area.

"Let's see now," Del had studied their faces, "you're Carol, you're Jack, you must be Linda, and you're . . ." he stopped short as his eyes fell on a tall, dark-haired youth whose dancing eyes and curly hair seemed vaguely familiar.

"I'm Richard," the youth announced clearly as he reached out his hand and shook Del's firmly. "You may not remember me."

"Oh, yes, I remember!" My husband returned the young man's grip and smile. Silently he asked, "How could I forget?"

Del had first learned of Richard and his family when I had written to him while he was in Canada:

> We had a new family in church Sunday. The mother seems to be well known to the congregation, but I had never seen her before. It seems that her husband, who has been repeatedly in and out of jail, left her when the twins were born, leaving her to care for her six children alone. Richard is the oldest—he is only nine. The twins are about the age of our baby. She brought them all the way across town on the bus. When I saw her struggling with the twins and another little boy scarcely more than a baby and remembered how my arms sometimes ache with

only one, I could not stand to see her start back to the bus line alone, so I invited them to the apartment for lunch. After lunch, our pastor who was visiting across the street, took them home in his car.

The next week there had been another letter:

> Our family was back in church today. Thor took them home this time, and he tells me they have a terrible place in which to live. From their clothing I would guess they are in need of some real help. When you get home, maybe we can go and see.

We had gone to see. Picking our way through the weeds and briars of the unkept lawn, we found the outside stairs to the back entrance to the semi-attic apartment, and inside to a very dingy makeshift home. Rags and cardboard had been used to repair broken windows. Wallpaper hung loosely from the ceiling and was shredded up the walls where little hands had found loose sections a handy plaything. The paint, where it could be identified as paint, was smoky and fingermarked. The floor, where there was no covering, was rough and splintery, the varnish long since worn away. On the kitchen floor there had been a linoleum, but the lacquered surface was worn completely away, leaving only the sticky tar base. No wonder Thor's shoes had stuck to the floor when he tried to walk across it. Both of us made mental notes of apparent needs as we visited.

The next week when the women's circle met, I told of this sister's need and proposed a plan that Del and I had designed for making those attic rooms a pleasant home. It received enthusiastic approval by the group.

So it was that, with the permission of the landlord and paint supplied by him, the young women of the congregation and their husbands papered and painted, scrubbed and sanded, varnished and polished, cleared away rubbish, and made windows whole. They had planned to replace the kitchen linoleum, but Richard's mother insisted that she could do that much on her own.

In a house that could be kept clean, the children immediately improved in appearance, and a radiant smile replaced the look of concern and embarrassment on the mother's face.

Following this, we made many calls at Richard's home, bringing encouragement, instruction, hope, and sometimes physical necessities. Before long the family moved to a larger home in an apartment building nearer the church. Many of the Saints took upon themselves the responsibility of providing transportation for the family to church and other needed services.

And now here was Richard, a handsome young man of ambition and promise, product of a courageous mother, a sympathetic congregation, and the gospel of Jesus Christ. How different his life might have been!

"What joy," Del mused, when the Leaguers had driven away, "to be engaged in a work with the Master who came to give life and to give it more abundantly!"

THE FIERY FURNACE

A subdued hum of activity pervaded the stake offices that bright winter morning. The sound of the steady rhythm of the typewriters touched by the skilled fingers of the secretaries sifted into the library which doubled as the seventy's office. The stake president had come in for a brief conference with the seventy and sat facing the spacious window which framed the view of the east lawn of the church grounds and the little city beyond. Suddenly an explosion shattered the morning's serenity.

"What was that?" Delbert and Herb Lively jumped to their feet simultaneously at the sharp retort that reverberated across the city. Together they ran to the window to see if there was evidence of the source of the sound.

"Look!" Del pointed excitedly to the smoke billowing from the still shuddering furnace room of the high school across the ravine and up the next hill from the church, "It's the school!" The two ministers raced for the car and hurried to the school.

"What happened? Was anybody hurt?" The questions were on the lips of every person who crowded the high school door.

"The furnace blew up. George Jardine was hurt bad!" There was an ominous hush over the group as they awaited the return of the ambulance crew that had already entered the building with the stretcher.

Earlier that morning George Jardine had entered the furnace room to investigate what appeared to be trouble with the boiler. The harsh hissing of steam rushing from the safety valve confirmed his fears that something was malfunctioning. Although the air fan had shut off, the natural gas used for fuel still gushed into the combustion chamber and burned there. Hastily climbing atop the boiler where the controls centered, George found and tripped the control that shut off the supply of gas. The cessation was only momentary, however. While the custodian was still on the boiler, the supply valve on the burner in front of the boiler opened, and again there was the hissing of gas as the red hot firebox filled with fuel. The gas buildup was already dangerously high, but the conscientious custodian knew that he must stop the gas from escaping or there would be a disastrous explosion that could cost the lives of numerous children and school personnel. Quickly he scurried from the top of the boiler to reach the one control that could avert such a catastrophe.

By now George had diagnosed the malfunction and knew exactly which mechanism he must reach to correct it. Knowing full well the danger involved, he resolutely squatted in front of the burner and leaned forward to reach the faulty apparatus. He was still working, bent directly over the danger area, when the unburned gas being fed into the firebox at high pressure ignited on the hot bricks.

The force of the blast blew off the firebox doors and George was enveloped in flame. There was a grizzly sizzling sound as George's straight white hair kinked under the heat and burned to a crisp rusty brown. To the smell of gas and smoke was added the sickening odor of burning flesh. His clothing, face, and hands aflame, George was thrown bodily against the boiler room wall. Fortunately a large piece of insulation hit him in the chest forcing him to exhale violently and protecting his lungs from the burning gas. Dazed and severely burned, the custodian slumped to the floor.

The pain was intense and there was no strength left in his body. Suddenly he felt arms close about him and he was gently half dragged, half carried through the smoke and debris toward the heavy fire door that separated the furnace room from the rest of the school. George was alone in the boiler room when the explosion occurred, and entrance could be gained only by sliding open the heavy steel self-closing door that weighed several hundred pounds. The door had not opened until his rescuer approached it bearing his body. Distinctly, then, he heard it open and close after him as his benefactor laid him carefully on the floor outside.

"Here he is!" someone cried. "Here in the storeroom!"

Among the first to reach the scene was the school principal. Seeing how badly burned he was, Mr. Booker, who was also a patriarch, dropped to his knees beside the stricken man. "George." He wasn't sure the injured man was conscious. "George," he repeated, "would you like for me to administer to you?"

The pain George suffered was too intense for him to speak, but he nodded faintly indicating that he understood.

Carefully the concerned minister poured oil on the charred head from the vial he always carried in his pocket, and touching the burned hair lightly so as not to add to the pain, he petitioned the heavenly Father for restoration to life and health.

"How did he get out here?" someone asked when the prayer was finished. "He couldn't have opened that heavy door by himself."

"Not with those hands!" another responded. "He would have left skin all over the place."

By now the fire department was quashing the fire, and the ambulance had arrived. One bystander, anxious to be helpful, reached out to lift the injured man to the stretcher. "My God!" The exclamation was really a prayer. The horrified man stood staring at his hands. Clinging to his fingers were patches of cooked skin that had come from George's burned arms when the volunteer touched them.

A gasp of horror rippled down the hall as the stretcher-bearers carried the semiconscious man toward the ambulance. Del noted that George's magnificent head of white hair now resembled a mass of rusty steel wool. His own flesh tingled at the sight of George's charred face, hands, and arms. Adelina Booker, wife of the patriarch-principal and school nurse, climbed into the ambulance to accompany the injured man to the hospital twenty-two miles away.

The word spread rapidly among the young students. "Let's go to the auditorium to pray for him!" "In the auditorium ... a prayer service." "Forget your lunch." "Pray for George!" The number grew as the word spread. Led by

Paul DeBarthe, a high school senior, the band of fasting students prayed earnestly for George's recovery.

When Delbert entered the hospital room to visit him the next day, George was awake, alert, and cheerful. Burned tissue had crusted about his mouth making it difficult for him to speak or smile. Relieved at finding him already so far on his way to recovery, Del teased him a little. "Do you know why you had that explosion?" he asked, feigning seriousness.

"No. Why?" George was unsuspecting.

"Because the Lord thought you needed more fire in your sermons," the seventy answered with a grin.

George grinned, too, painfully! "I'll get even with you!" he retorted when the pain had subsided and he could straighten his face. He well knew Delbert's high regard for his sermons by the number of times my husband requested his services in areas where good evangelistic preaching was needed.

George, a priest, was also teacher of the church school class I attended. He missed two Sundays, but on the third he appeared unshaven and apologetic. "You'll have to excuse me." He smiled broadly as he addressed the class. "I'm in the process of reconstruction." A month later he was back at work full time, bearing only minor scars as a result of his ordeal.

"They're saying he was not badly burned," Adelina confided to me when we were discussing George's miraculous recovery one day. "I rode with him in the ambulance. I *know* how badly he was burned. This is the Lord's doing!"

FLIGHT OF JOY

The fleeing woman paused long enough to close the stair door softly, then resumed her flight down the deserted street of the county seat town. It was Sunday morning and the few cars in sight belonged to residents of the second-floor apartments above the business houses that lined the courthouse square or to the Saints who met each Lord's day in the hall above Dick's Music Store. There were no pedestrians on the deserted street except the little grey-haired woman who ran uncertainly toward the residential area off the square.

"Why did Helen rush out of the service like that before we were finished?" Delbert turned to the pastor, perplexed by the strange behavior of the one person in his Sunday morning congregation who was not a member of Christ's church. "I felt the Good Spirit in my preaching. Surely I didn't offend her! I certainly hope I didn't!"

Early that summer morning we crossed the state line to join the small group of Saints who had not yet obtained their own meeting place for worship. After the classes were finished, Del preached. Just as he concluded his sermon, the demure little maiden lady arose hastily from her back-row seat at the side of the long narrow hall in which the congregation met, grabbed her purse and Bible from the floor, and hurried out the door and down the long stairs that led to the street. Never before in the many years this nonmember friend of the church had attended the little mission had she behaved so strangely.

"Was Helen ill?" Del inquired of the friend with whom Helen had come to the meeting.

"Not that I know of." The friend was puzzled too.

All day Del tried unsuccessfully to remember something he had said or done that might have offended the sensitive little woman. In no way could he account for her actions until Tuesday's mail brought him a letter.

"I want to apologize for beating such a hasty retreat Sunday," Helen explained.

It seemed that she had spent many years enjoying the fellowship of the Saints but seriously questioning a number of their beliefs. On this particular morning, Delbert had answered her questions one by one without previous knowledge of her questioning.

"And what's more," she wrote reverently, "I knew before you spoke them, every word of your sermon."

It was such an unusual and exhilarating experience that Helen was overwhelmed by it. "I had to jump up and shout or cry or do something," she wrote, "and I decided you wouldn't want me to make a commotion in the church. So I ran home where I could make all the fuss I wanted!

"I'd like to have you and Brother Judson come to see me this week," she concluded, "and I think you know what I want to see you about."

Helen and a number of other candidates were baptized in Big G Lake on the Graceland campus during reunion. Joyfully she made her covenant with her Lord and Savior who had reached out to her in a most remarkable fashion to assure her of her worth. Soon thereafter she took her place in the mission congregation as a church school teacher, sharing generously the richness of her testimony.

NO FUNERAL FOR ANDY

The heat of the midwestern August sun dispersed the crowds quickly. Clusters of people gathered under the abundant shade trees on the reunion grounds. Delbert stood near the door of the assembly room greeting Saints from all over the stake as they left the service. Momentarily he gazed past the heads of those about him and spotted a family seated on a bench in the shade of a nearby oak waiting to see him. He signaled his recognition of the group and finished greeting those about him.

"Andy! Andy Gwin! How good it is to see you!" Del hurried to the shaded area and grasped the outstretched hand of the small, red-haired man whose freckled face beamed his own appreciation of this moment with the seventy.

"Believe me, it's good to be here!" Andy responded fervently. "They say I almost didn't make it!"

"You certainly almost didn't!" Del responded heartily, and his memory re-created those uncertain hours of a few weeks before.

Del had been scheduled to minister that Sunday in the little white church recently acquired by the congregation of which the Gwins were a part. Late Saturday Cleo Boswell, who pastored the congregation from some forty miles away, called to inform the seventy of Andy's need for ministry. The man had suffered a heart attack as he repaired his roof; the resultant fall complicated his already serious condition.

"Why don't you folk and our family take a lunch?" Cleo proposed. "After church we will eat in a park where the children can play while we go to the hospital to see what we can do to help." We agreed.

At the hospital, however, we were denied entry into Andy's room. "No one can go in to see him." The receptionist was firm in her refusal.

"Not even his ministers?" Del asked in surprise. From experience he knew that Dorothy and I would not mind being left behind if only the men could be admitted. "This man is his pastor, and I, too, am a minister."

"The doctor left orders," the receptionist explained patiently. "He says Mr. Gwin is so ill that the excitement of one unexpected person could bring instant death."

"Then may we see his family?" This was certainly no time to be insistent.

The receptionist pointed across the lobby. "You will find them there in that private room."

Inside the room the family had gathered, solemn-faced and silent, to await Andy's death. The two ministers saw at a glance a real need for ministry here even though they could not be admitted to the sick man's room.

"It looks pretty bad." Del reached out to take Sister Gwin's trembling hands into his own strong, comforting fingers.

"The doctor says there is no hope." The dejected woman bit her lip to try to quell the tears that rushed into being at the sight of her minister friends. "They have him in an oxygen tent, but even then he is barely conscious most of the time. He can neither eat nor drink. They let me be with him, and they let him see the children for a moment this afternoon, but only because he can't live much longer."

"Even though we can't go into the room to administer to him," Del proposed, "we can have prayer for him here. Let's gather into a circle. I will pray first and whoever wishes may follow. Brother Boswell will close our prayer."

Just to be doing something relieved the tension of the waiting. Earnest prayers were offered in behalf of the man who lay so near death in the room down the hall.

As the prayers closed, Andy's wife spoke with the two ministers. "Will you help me plan the funeral?" she asked with resignation. "We want Cleo to preach the sermon, and you, Delbert, to conduct the service."

"Of course, we will," my husband assured her, looking at Cleo for confirmation of his acceptance of the requested assignment. "But let's not be in too much of a hurry. There was a good Spirit here as we offered our prayers. Let's give God a chance to answer them."

The hour grew late and Delbert knew that we must get home so he could fill his evening appointment. The Boswells, however, were reluctant to leave. "I think we'll wait an hour or so...," the concerned pastor asserted.

"Then come by the house," Del requested, "and tell us how he is."

"Of course," Cleo agreed, and the two men exchanged glances that stirred a tremor of hope in everyone who saw it.

An hour after we reached home, the Boswells entered our drive. Del heard them coming and hurried out the door to greet them.

"How is he?" he questioned eagerly.

"Sitting on his bed eating supper when I left!" Cleo reported happily. "Andy is going to be all right!"

"Thank God!" Del said fervently.

* * * * *

"It was good of you to come to the hospital." Andy's thanks recalled Delbert to the campgrounds.

"Did your wife tell you about that funeral service we almost planned for you?" Del bantered.

"Thought she'd be rid of me there for a while, didn't she? Well, I sure fooled her!" Andy joined in the fun as he drew his smiling wife to him in a brief embrace.

"Yeah," the seventy agreed, "you and the Lord!"

THE IMPOSSIBLE BORDER CROSSING

"This is the camera." Del pointed out the equipment in the trunk of his car to the inspector at the Aduana.

"Correcto!" replied the wide-eyed official.

"This is the projector that shows pictures," the seventy continued to point.

"Correcto!" responded the official.

"This is the speaker—you know, it makes the sound that goes with the pictures." Del wanted to make sure the function of the equipment was understood.

"Correcto!"

Months earlier the Fishburns had left the valuable movie equipment and stacks of film on the States side of the Mexican border. It was all a part of Bob's inheritance from his father and would be extremely valuable to him as a seventy doing missionary work in Mexico once it could be taken into the country. To pay duty on it, however, would cost a small fortune.

"I don't know how to get it across the border," Bob had said when he left it. "We'll just have to leave it here until we can find a way."

Many a trip had been made across the border since that

day, but none of the church officials, visitors to the mission, or even the Fishburns themselves would attempt to take the movies or their paraphernalia.

We had agreed to make the trip to Saltillo to take Olive Kon from Hawaii to the student center which the Fishburns directed in that city of schools. Olive thought she might be of some assistance in the operation of the center.

When plans were first made for the trip, Delbert had suggested taking the movies and equipment, but serious consideration of the problems involved had caused him to reject the idea. "Maybe we could take just one item," he had finally decided before the family had retired for the night. "If we cannot get it through we will just have to drive back and leave it here on this side of the border until we return."

"Mildred... are you awake?" It was three in the morning when Del began to call my name.

"What is it?" I asked sleepily.

"We're going to take the whole outfit."

"What?" I was alert now, though uncomprehending.

"I have been praying about all of that movie equipment," he responded. "Bob could really make good use of it in his work down there. We're going to take it all!"

"But how?" I was not convinced.

"Just put it into the car and tell the border officials what it is." Del was obviously positive that, fantastic as it seemed, the plan would work.

"All right, if you say so." There may have been a trace of awe in my voice. Certainly I knew that my husband had some assurance that his unbelievable idea was valid.

"What about the Christmas gifts that came last week for the Fishburns?" If all that valuable apparatus could go, there didn't seem to be much reason to make the family wait for their gifts.

"We'll take them, too."

"Are you sure?" I peered quizzically at my husband.

"I'm sure," he replied simply.

Hours later, with the trip well under way, Del was explaining his load and his plan to Elder George Colbath, an experienced border-crosser who was making the trip as interpreter and guide for us.

"Oh, no! Whatever possessed you to think you could do that?" Elder Colbath was distressed at Del's seeming naïvete. He was sure the border guards would insist on a heavy duty. "You can't possibly do it! We had better turn around right now and unload before we try the border."

"No," Del affirmed, "we will take the load in."

He then explained how much Bob needed the equipment, how the idea for taking it in had been impressed upon his mind as he prayed for direction, and his confidence that God would open the way for a successful conclusion to the mission.

Elder Colbath shook his head in consternation. Although he believed in prayer, this was just too much to ascribe to God.

* * * * *

Now they were at the border undergoing their first inspection.

"Correcto! Correcto! Correcto!" the puzzled official surveyed each item as Delbert pointed it out. With a nod and a gesture of resignation he motioned the men into the Aduana. I offered a silent prayer that there would be no delay. In minutes they returned triumphantly bearing the official papers that permitted their entry into Mexico. Their precious cargo was undisturbed and untaxed.

"That was unbelievable!" Elder Colbath was delighted. We were jubilant.

"There are two more checkpoints." Elder Colbath knew we were not yet in free.

"There are?" Del had supposed the border crossing would be final.

"Why should that bother you?" Elder Colbath could not resist a little teasing when he noted a note of concern in Del's voice.

"It shouldn't," my husband agreed. "With a beginning like that, how could anyone doubt the ending."

Twice more the routine was followed: "This is a camera." "Correcto!" "This is a projector." "Correcto!" and on through the entire movie outfit.

"And what is that?" the Inspector pointed to the box of gifts.

"Those are Christmas gifts for the Fishburn family," Del explained without moving to open the gifts.

"Correcto!" came the response, and the last official waved us past the final point of inspection.

"Bob, I have something for you," Del announced when greetings and introductions were finished at the mission house. "Come and see." With a flourish he opened the trunk of the car.

Bob was speechless! He passed his hand over his face to make sure he was actually seeing the items before him. Then he sputtered, "How? What? Why, they would have me in jail for three months if I had even tried to cross the border with all that. How on earth did you manage?"

Gratefully Del recounted his prayer and the assurance by divine direction of the way.

CARMEN, CHILD OF DIGNITY

Beautiful days are not rare in the Valley of the Rio Grande River, and this early Sunday morning promised to be one of the most lovely of all. But Carmen seemed not to see the shimmering beauty of the orange blossoms, or smell their fragrance, or feel the soft breeze that stirred her glistening auburn hair as she stood at our door. She had come unusually early this morning. Services at the church would not start for another hour or more.

Seeing the troubled look in the girl's eyes, I throttled my own exuberant greeting to ask solicitously, "How are things this morning, Carmen?"

"Okay, I guess," came the evasive reply.

"No, really," I insisted, "how are things with you?"

"Okay." The dejected teen-ager shifted her shoulders, not so much to shrug off the question as to shift the burden that weighed so heavily on them.

"Oh, I guess." She swallowed hard. "I just don't feel anything anymore. Everything hurts, but nothing hurts!" Quickly the young Latin American turned away, hoping her averted face would hide the depth of despair that clouded her deep brown eyes.

Concern welled up in my heart.

"Oh, Carmen, my poor dear Carmen!" I cried inside with love and pity I dared not express. Aloud I questioned gently, "Want to tell me about it?"

I knew well much of the story Carmen would tell if she really "told me about it." But I also knew that there would be little said. I could only pray that there would be some ministry for her that morning at the church.

* * * * *

It had been almost a year now since I had met Carmen. I had first seen her standing on one foot, slouched beside her family's crude, floorless hovel sucking on an orange and looking so defiant that I had almost despaired of ever becoming her friend. I had gone to the Perez home with Ana Maria who stood several feet in front of me speaking in Spanish to Carmen's mother explaining my presence.

It had been shortly before Christmas, and the women of the church had wanted to share their Christmas with a needy family, but there had been no needy families in the congregation. Even the poorer members seemed to have found the strength, encouragement, direction, and assistance to make life more productive and satisfying. So Ana, a recent convert and a nurse, had volunteered the name of Carmen's mother as one in dire need of help, and I had come to meet her and offer that assistance.

Celia Perez had needed assistance. She had been ill, and Ana had been going regularly to inject the medicine that was bringing her back to health. Juan Perez had died a few months before, victim of a highway accident. "The Lord put His finger on him," Carmen later had told me, "so that Mother and I could have some peace." Night after night he had come home from work drunk and penniless.

Because there would be neither sufficient food nor a decent place to sleep, Juan would respond to his own hatred for himself by beating his wife and frightening his children.

Besides Carmen, there were mischievous Ferdinand with the winning smile, barrel-chested Junior whose deformity bespoke some as yet undiagnosed illness, and little Maria whose long curls and shy smile quickly captivated the visitor's heart. All of these had to be Carmen's responsibility when her mother was able to work.

When she could, Mrs. Perez would walk to the corner cafe on the highway and work ten hours a day, for thirty-five cents an hour—$24.50 if she got in a full week, but with her illness she rarely got more than $17.00. When reminded that the minimum wage required by law was $1.25 an hour, her employer would only shrug and suggest that she quit; there were plenty of others who would be glad to make the thirty-five cents!

Juan had accumulated enough credit to provide Social Security benefits for Celia and the children—slightly more than one hundred dollars monthly. From it, she had to repay the debts that Juan had left at the bank, pay the mortician who had buried him, and make the payments on the lot on which she hoped someday to have a real home instead of the deteriorating cabañas that now occupied the space. And, of course, there was interest. It seemed the poorer one was the higher the rate of interest.

Ana had talked to Celia in Spanish for a long time. I had been able to understand just enough to know that she had assured her of the sincerity of the churchwomen and their desire to help. She had also told her a little about the church and her newfound faith.

As I waited I glanced around the yard. The ground was bare of grass or weeds. Evidently someone wanted it that way. A lovely cactus garden filled the southwest corner, and a hot pepper bush separated the cactus from the beans and squash that were planted along the fence. A mesquite tree sprawled across the front yard, and an orange tree grew in the back. There were two buildings. "One looks like our old smokehouse," I reminisced, "and the other looks like a miniature of the makeshift barn that served to shelter our livestock until we could build a real one." Both of these were floorless, and neither had ever been painted. Actually there were three buildings. The third was the privy that stood at the end of a string of rough boards laid across the garden to make a path.

For the building that served as the main house, Juan had set posts in the ground and nailed on rough boards like those that now made the path through the garden. On my second visit I was invited inside. There I saw a partition of tin roofing and cardboard boxes that separated the kitchen from the area in which there was a bed. There was an old divan near the door. An ancient treadle sewing machine, the prized possession of the household, stood across from the divan. Both were laden with piles of unironed clothes.

There were cracks between the boards that made up the walls and between the walls and the tin roof. These were stuffed with newspaper and old rags during the winter and sometimes when it rained. Screen wire covered the front end of the building, but there were neither windows nor shutters to close in case of a storm. Now that it was winter, ragged old blankets were hung in front to help keep out the cold wind.

A bucket of charcoal burned dully in the center of the room to help dispel the chill from the air. Even though it seldom froze in the Valley, and despite the fact that winter was the season for the harvest of oranges and grapefruit, the blossoming of the most gorgeous flowers and the planting of the best gardens, the temperature through many days was far below the comfort level.

For cooking there was a kerosene stove. There was no gas, no electricity, no water—except from a faucet that came up out of the ground beside the cactus garden.

The second building, which had served as a bedroom when Juan was alive, now housed only a wardrobe containing the family's best clothing.

I had loved Celia from the start. I had found her

intelligent, sweet, and beautiful. The classic features of her sunbrowned face with its high cheekbones and well turned nose gave testimony to her Indian heritage, while the errant curls framing her face and her thick, glistening braid spoke of her Spanish ancestry. Although she could neither read nor write she spoke English quite well, but preferred her native Spanish tongue.

When Ana Maria had asked about the family's needs, Carmen had declared, "I don't need anything for Christmas." She had spoken sullenly without removing the orange completely from her lips. "Sure don't want any clothes!" One glance at the huge pile of cast-off clothing that already cluttered the main room of the house had given me ample evidence of the reason for her firmness on this point. "She has already been hurt by would-be benefactors," I observed silently. "I wonder if we will ever be able to reach her." I longed to take the plump fourteen-year-old in my arms and soothe away the hurt.

There were no secondhand clothes in the Christmas basket for the Perez family. There wasn't even a turkey, for they had no oven in which to bake one and no refrigerator in which to preserve leftovers. Even Carmen responded with warmth when they were escorted to the Christmas service, and she sang beautifully the familiar Christmas carols. Both she and her mother were surprised to find other people of Mexican descent in the congregation participating with the Anglos in the services and social activities that followed. This was more than an offering of castaways and a box of food. This was an offer of friendship and love to which the needy family responded gratefully. Carmen was especially responsive; soon she was a regular visitor at our home and a participant in the activities of the church.

Intimate talks with Carmen had given me much to admire of Celia's principles and teachings. Many an evening Carmen would stay at our home past nightfall, helping wash the dishes and tidy up the house or playing with the children.

On these occasions, unwilling to let her walk alone in the dark across the railroad tracks and past the vegetable sheds, I would walk her home. During these walks I learned how, in spite of their poverty, Celia had taught her children to be strictly honest. I learned also of their humble faith in God. They didn't understand him, but they loved and respected him. I learned of the simple pride the family shared in the well kept yard and garden that surrounded their dwellings and in the dirt floor swept clean of debris and sprinkled often to keep down the dust.

"Mother says I never need to be ashamed of my home as long as it is neat and clean," Carmen told me one night when we talked of the relationship of teen-age daughters to their mothers.

"Your mother is a wonderful woman," I said. "You're a lucky girl!"

There were questions about Social Security, and we went with Celia to see that she was getting the maximum available to her. When Del was around with the car, we drove the family to church. When there was food left over from camp or a church supper, we saw to it that Celia got a share of the supplies. One day an envious neighbor offered, "I'll join your church if you'll bring me things like you bring Celia." I didn't bother to explain that Celia was not a member of the church.

At Easter, we took Carmen to the store and let her choose an Easter dress—a beautiful black and white checked suit with a rich yellow blouse. She looked lovely in it. After the first laundering, however, I spotted it in the pile of unironed clothes. Week after week it remained there. Finally I understood. How stupid I had been not to realize that the clothers were never ironed for there was no way to iron them! I helped rejuvenate the dress.

One day there was a beautiful crocheted chair set spread out on the old divan when I arrived for a visit. The pattern was executed skillfully in yellows and brown. I rarely used doilies, but I did admire this handicraft.

"How beautiful!" I exclaimed. "Did you make it, Celia?"

"Oh, yes!" she beamed. "And I'm glad you like it. I did it for you."

"Oh, no," I protested, "you can sell it and make a lot of money."

Celia smiled broadly as she shook her head emphatically. "For you, Sister Smith. For you!"

I accepted the precious offering with tear-filled eyes. What a woman!

"I have something else to show you." Celia beamed with happiness. "See!" and she pulled a large book from a new box at the end of the divan. An old rag rug had been carefully placed beneath the container to make sure it did not touch the tamped earth. "I bought Carmen a set of encyclopedia."

"Encyclopedia!" I exclaimed, and immediately hoped Celia would not detect the consternation in my voice.

"Uh huh!" The happy woman nodded, trembling with excitement. "It cost me three hundred dollars, but I only have to pay ten dollars a month," she explained.

"Carmen will like that," I agreed, wondering where on earth Celia would find another ten dollars a month for the payment. I was really angry with any salesman who dared to convince a woman so poor that she needed such an expensive item. How would she keep it from being rained on or chewed by the rats and mice that roamed at will over the property? Could it possibly be that it was bought at least partly to please us—to prove to us that she was really interested in Carmen's future, too? The thought made me a little ill.

One night an errand took me on a later-than-usual visit to

the crude structure that housed the struggling little family. It was after suppertime, but Celia was in her kitchen making tortillas. I watched with fascination as the skilled brown hands dipped into the dough cradled in a beautiful pottery bowl. I had never seen such a bowl. It was fully two feet in diameter; the sides sloped gently, like a giant saucer, and the inside was covered with an intricately executed design in which greens and blues predominated. Shadows cast by the kerosene lamp that burned dimly on the oilcloth-covered table played about the bowl's tapestry and danced whimsically against the slanting rooftop-ceiling of the enclosure as Celia's nimble fingers lifted the dough, rolled it expertly into balls, and skillfully flattened them into round tortillas ready for the hot iron griddle that covered the flickering kerosene fire. On the other burner of the two-burner stove a pot of water was beginning to steam for the *cafe* (coffee) soon to be boiled.

The lamp lighted not only the faces of Celia and her children, who stood on tiptoe peering hungrily over the partition from the foot of the bed in the next room, their bodies blended into the shadows that the feeble light could not penetrate, but also revealed the form of a man hunched forward from a low stool in the right-hand corner of the kitchen. He was apparently waiting for the tortillas to be baked and may have been in conversation with the woman before I was bidden to enter the room. He did not turn to acknowledge my presence, and I could not see his face in the dim light. His presence was that of an immovable dark shadow hovering near the food.

Celia lifted the beautiful bowl to make way for a plate for the freshly baked tortillas. As she momentarily held it in her arms, I watched transfixed at the exquisite picture they made and for a moment yearned to be an artist capable of putting it on canvas for all of the world to admire. I made a mental note to look for such a bowl the next time I visited the markets across the border in Mexico to have the object to enhance the memory when the moment had passed.

The man was Mr. Moreno, Celia explained on my next visit, and he wanted her to marry him. His wife was dead, his family grown, and he had the big truck (that was now frequently parked outside Celia's gate) with which to make a lot of money. After he began visiting her Celia quit walking to the highway to work in the cafe. "He is a good man, and he loves my children," she repeated again and again as though it was necessary to convince me—or herself—of the truthfulness of the assertion. And the "proof" of Mr. Moreno's love lay all about—a brand-new bicycle for Carmen, an expensive pedal car for Ferdinand, a radio-record player for Maria, and a tricycle for Junior.

But Mr. Moreno didn't really want to marry Celia. He just wanted the privileges of marriage while he camouflaged the discharge of his responsibilities with incongruously lavish presents for the children. And Carmen was troubled. Again she was hearing the sounds of lovemaking in the night in the crowded hovel with the dirt floor and the cardboard partitions without doors. Only now it was her mother—who had always been so good and who had taught her about God and right and honor and love—who was breaking the commandments which Carmen had been taught to obey. It was her mother whom she had protected so fiercely from the blows of her own father's heavy hands and for whom she had prayed so fervently who now, it seemed to her, had turned her back on the God who she believed had set his hand to bring her peace. It was more than Carmen could bear alone.

* * * * *

Now at Communion service as I sat beside Carmen participating in the pageantry of the service, my heart went out to the lonely girl beside me. "Oh, God," I prayed, "Touch Carmen with your loving Spirit. Help her to know that she does not bear her pain alone. Help us to teach her and her mother your will and way that there shall yet be joy in their lives and in their home." Gently I reached out and touched Carmen in a gesture of love and understanding graced by the Spirit of God that flowed abundantly over the congregation at that moment.

The service was over. Carmen no longer slumped beneath the weight of her fears. Her dark eyes sparkled, and her smile shone from a radiance that reached deep within her soul. Or was it the reflection of the Master of Men who had touched her with love and understanding and assurance?

"It's all right now!" Carmen nodded jubilantly. "The weight's all gone. I feel so much better now I think I can go home."

CARMEN, VICTIM OF PERFIDY

When Hurricane Beulah devastated the Valley, the storm was too much for the fragile home of the Perez family. One-hundred-and-twenty-five-mile-an-hour winds ripped off sheets of the tin roofing and left them strewn about the neighborhood. Torrents of rain flooded the well-beaten dirt floors, turning them into puddles of mire. Fear gripped my heart as I viewed the desolate area.

As soon as the storm had passed and civil defense authorities had permitted anyone other than authorized personnel in the streets, I rushed to see how Celia and her family had fared. Mentally I chastised myself for not asking them to move to our sturdy old home when the storm warnings came. But this was the first hurricane I had experienced, and I really did not know what to expect.

The last time there had been a hurricane warning fifteen frightened people had taken shelter in the mission house, but nothing had happened to justify their fears, and I had expected this to be a similar situation. This time Delbert was a hundred and fifty miles up the coast, and I had assured him that there was no need to leave his work to come home ... the children and I would be all right. I had expected the storm to come to a limited area and pass swiftly like the midwestern tornadoes with which I was familiar. I had not counted on the hours of torrential rain whipped for miles by howling winds and flooding vast acreages.

"Celia," I called at the door of the tattered main house. There was no reply. Only the sodden divan that still held the cast-off clothing and some rain-filled boxes of refuse that were falling apart remained in the abandoned structure. I looked for the encyclopedia, hoping the precious books had escaped damage. They were nowhere to be seen. In the other house, footprints in the mud of the once well-tamped floor bore mute evidence of the conditions of last occupancy. The good clothing was gone from the wardrobe, however. That must mean the family was safe somewhere.

Though I knew it was useless, I called again and again, "Celia! Celia!" Finally giving up the hopeless quest, I picked my way across the debris that littered the yard and called to the neighbor on the west.

"Uncle Jake!" Carmen had introduced me weeks before to the venerable Negro who now sat on his front porch nodding over his pipe, and we always exchanged greetings when we were in the neighborhood. "Do you know where Celia and the children are?"

Uncle Jake knew and I was relieved to learn that some of Juan's relatives had taken them into their own tiny house before the hurricane had struck.

"How did you come through the storm?" I inquired solicitously.

"Pretty good," the old man responded thankfully, "but we did spring some leaks. Would you like to see?"

Carefully I picked my way through the cactus garden to the little cottage graced with ivy and morning glories on the porch posts and cared for so tenderly by the aging couple who resided there. Happy to have someone with whom he could discuss their problem, the tottering old man rose to lead the way inside where we surveyed their damage and I learned more of Celia's situation.

The Red Cross had offered seventy-five dollars to help Celia fix the roof of the hovel, but she had decided the time had come for her children to have a floor under their feet. She tried unsuccessfully to get financing to build the home of which she had dreamed so long. None was available.

But Mr. Moreno found a house—one long room with a wall-high partition dividing it into a living room, bedroom, and lean-to kitchen. Once it had been painted white, but now it was a nondescript grey. A rickety porch clung perilously to the front. Although it was smaller than the hovel had been, it had a floor and windows and a door to keep out the rain. Here, too, were electric lights, a sink with running water, and gas for cooking. Into the tiny house, Mr. Moreno had moved the desperate family with promises that the new house they dreamed of would be built on the old lot. Now his visits became more and more frequent and extended, and he began to assume the disciplinary role of a father in the home.

At first Carmen had tried to show her mother how she felt. When Mr. Moreno stayed well past the bedtime hour and when it was apparent that there would be more disquieting sounds during the night, Carmen got on her bicycle and rode and rode and rode, coming by her house frequently to see if her mother was yet alone.

One night she had ridden until she was nearly exhausted. Well past midnight the truck was still in front of the house. In desperation, the girl sought out her paternal grandmother's home and spent the rest of the night there.

But her mother did not hear what her frantic daughter was saying, and with the urging of Mr. Moreno she called the police and charged her with flagrant disobedience. They testified that she had been frequenting the beer parlor against her mother's instruction, which was illegal for one of her age, and Carmen was sent to the county jail. All weekend she was held in jail and on into Monday. Only her persistent insistence that she must be in school had finally prevailed upon the authorities to release her into her grandmother's custody.

"Why didn't you have them call us?" we questioned, horrified at the experience of one so young.

"I didn't want to bother you," she replied simply. "Do you know they are going to send me to the reform school?" she continued, and the resignation in her voice was almost that of relief.

"Oh, no, they are not!" Del vowed fervently. "Not as long as we are here, they aren't! May we go talk to your mother? Perhaps we can help her understand."

"You know she is going to have a baby?" Carmen's question was a statement of hopelessness. Now her place in the home had been totally usurped by Mr. Moreno. With his baby coming and the other children dependent on him, Carmen had no hope of returning.

We did go to talk to Celia, only to be met with total rejection of our pleas for Carmen. "She is a wicked girl!" Celia had declared. "She smokes and drinks beer and will not obey Mr. Moreno. And he is a *good* man. He loves my children!"

"We'll believe he is a good man, Celia, the day he marries you and gives his child his name!" I had blurted out, perhaps unwisely.

"Why do you insist that Carmen smokes and drinks beer when she does not?" Del had asked.

"Mr. Moreno says she does," Celia replied, and it was apparent that she dare not believe otherwise.

We next went to the authorities and inquired about Carmen and what was still in store for her as a result of the charge against her. "We have investigated, and there is no truth to the charge that she has been frequenting the beer parlor," the officers informed us. "We will just drop the charge."

"But that will not end her problems," Del insisted, and the situation that existed in the home was explained.

"You have proof that there is adultery being practiced in the home?" the officer questioned.

"There is a baby on the way," Del responded, "and the woman's husband has been dead for more than a year."

The officer nodded. "We will see that Carmen is not jailed again."

"But she needs someplace to live," Del persisted.

"Maybe her grandmother will keep her. If she will, we will leave her there."

For the first time in her life, Carmen had a beautiful home in which to live. The block house boasted two small bedrooms and a bath besides the living room, dining room, and kitchen. The polished oak floors shone with the loving care given them. Potted plants and tasteful knickknacks decorated the open shelf divider between the living room and dining room. There was a radio and even a small TV. Outside a chain link fence insured the privacy of the family and gave running room for the pet dog. The grassy lawn was tended carefully and blossomed with well chosen shrubs and flowers.

But there was little money in the Perez household—hardly enough to feed those already domiciled there, let alone provide for the needs of another. Grandmother Perez had to depend on the money she could save from her work in the fields during the vegetable season and the little that her daughters could contribute from their own sporadic jobs to keep the household operating since the death of her husband whose industry had provided the small but lovely home. There was little food, and no money at all for school supplies and incidentals needed by a fifteen-year-old.

Then I remembered the Social Security that was regularly going to Celia. Some of that was for Carmen's support. Perhaps there would be a way for it to be transferred to the grandmother. I made the appointment with the Social Security personnel only to learn that such a transfer of funds would require Celia's consent. So another appointment was made to which I brought Celia. The transfer was made. It was less than twenty dollars a month, but it would help supply needed notebooks, pencils, and clothing with a little for food.

Although she had transferred the Social Security funds without protest, Celia was not content to leave her daughter in her grandmother's home. It was almost time for her baby to be born. The birth would mean that she would need more help at home... and more money. Besides, Grandmother was a Catholic, and no daughter of hers should ever be reared a Catholic! With inconsistent logic, she purchased a set of supplements to the encyclopedia to lure her daughter back home. For some obscure reason, Mr. Moreno also made friendly overtures. He promised to teach Carmen how to drive and even to give her a car if she would come home.

Although the gift car never did materialize, Carmen did

return home. The baby was born, and Carmen loved it. It was easier now to accept her mother's new way of life. Maybe it was not so bad to break the commandments of God after all. Surely nothing could be wrong with producing such beauty, such innocence.

"You should have another baby," she said to me one day as we sat on the edge of the couch that doubled as her bed at night.

"That would be nice," I affirmed, "if there was money to care for it and educate it. I think the five we have may keep us quite busy. If there's any left over, maybe we can help some others like you."

Carmen was mystified. Wasn't just having a beautiful baby to play with and love justification enough for having it? The need to be loyal to her mother, who had so long been her ideal, had won out over the sense of right and wrong which had been taught to her by that same mother who now violated her own teaching.

CARMEN, MOTHER OF ELENA

We were fearful for Carmen's future, but the letter from church headquarters had decreed a move for us. Del was to return to school for a year, and we must be in Missouri by September. We had spent many hours talking with her about her life and God's concern for her happiness. We helped her recall the times He had brought her help and hope when there seemed to be no way out for her. We taught her the scriptures that assured her that anyone fully committed to his way of life had nothing to fear. We tried to help her understand what he meant when he said, "I, the Lord, am bound when ye do what I say, but when ye do not what I say, ye have no promise."

Del had counseled her about her own chastity. Carmen was no longer a plump youngster. Her childish fat had given way to the graceful form and figure of a beautiful young woman. When she did her auburn hair up, she looked older than she really was and would be desired by many a man. Del had cautioned her about accepting the promises of men whom he knew would, in the environment in which she lived, ask her to give up her virginity. Both of us urged her to continue her schooling to prepare for a good job. There was nothing more we could do except to love her, pray for her, ask the other Saints to look after her, and keep in touch with her by mail.

"I am back in school again," the neatly written letter read, "and I'm doing so much better. You were right. Every day I ask God to help me, and every day He does help me." I read the letter gratefully. I had wondered, now that we had moved away, whether Carmen would carry through with her resolve to enter the technical school for job training. With the letter grasped in my hand, I relaxed in my chair and reminisced about another time Carmen had almost dropped out of school.

"I failed!" Carmen almost whispered the terrible word. "I failed, and Mama says I'm too dumb to go to school any more."

"Dumb!" The word fairly exploded from my surprised lips. "Carmen, you didn't fail because you're dumb. You failed because you had problems, dear ... just more problems than you could cope with. You can't quit now!"

I had known some of her problems—the poverty, the long

sleepless nights waiting with Mama for the return of her drunken father. The fearful, cringing, awful waiting huddled deep in the skimpy covers while her father beat her mother, heaping insults, accusations, and profanity upon her, hoping she would not be next but feeling guilty that she could not protect her mother—and the hurt when she tried. The days fighting sleep at her desk—a fight she frequently didn't win. The severe discipline from misunderstanding teachers and derision from the other students. The breakfastless mornings when there was not time to eat even if there was food. It was difficult to get out of bed after only a few hours rest from the time the shouting and beating had subsided, and often the brief span was filled with sounds of sexual gratification which made her uncomfortable and ashamed because she felt she was intruding.

Things had been better after her father's death, but years of failure are not easy to make up in a few months.

It was not until the Sunday after the report of Carmen's failure that I found out about her glasses. We had gone with several other church families to a beautiful cafeteria for lunch. Knowing that the girl had never before eaten in a cafeteria of this nature we invited her to join us. As we stood in line I pointed across the line of people moving slowly past the counter to the listing of foods and their prices displayed in large letters. "There," I explained, "is a list of all of the foods. Pick out what you want now and get it as we pass down the line."

Carmen was silent a moment, and her eyes narrowed almost to a slit as she squinted and leaned across the rail that separated the two lines of people. "But I can't see the words," she explained finally. "I broke my glasses."

"How did you do that?" I questioned.

"I fell on the skate board," she confessed shyly.

"At our house?" I was trying to recall how long it had

been since the children had played with the skate boards.

"Uh huh." Carmen nodded uncomfortably.

"I wonder why the children didn't say anything about it." I was concerned that I had not known.

"They were in my pocket," Carmen explained. "I didn't tell anybody."

"But why did you not tell us?"

"It was the Lion's Club," she explained, "that was so good to give me my glasses. I did not want the people who belong to it to think I did not care for them. And Mama can't buy me a new pair yet."

On Monday I went to school and talked to the principal, the counselor, and the school nurse, explaining Carmen's problem. For more than two months the frightened young girl had been unable to see clearly the blackboard, or the maps, or the instructions, or even the words in her texts or tests. Arrangements were made to get new glasses and for Carmen to make up the failed grades. Thus she returned to school.

* * * * *

After the first letter, mail began to come from another town—up north. "I'm here with my grandmother," Carmen said. "We're working in the fields." There were letters about the Jehovah's Witnesses and their efforts to convert the field hands. Carmen even offered to spend some of her wages to send us a New World translation of the Bible. That called for a long letter explaining that we not only had a New World translation of the Bible but that we had studied carefully other teachings of the Jehovah's Witnesses and had found them to be at variance with the scriptures. We also told her she would find it necessary to discard her beloved Book of Mormon if she espoused the Witness faith. Although Carmen had never asked for baptism, she believed and loved the book of her ancestors to which Christ's church had introduced her.

After the exchange of correspondence concerning Witnesses, there was a long silence from Carmen. Then came the explanation for the absence from school, the work in the fields, and the lack of mail. "I have a baby," she said. "I'm not sure how it happened."

Coming into the house of her mother unexpectedly one evening Carmen had overheard her mother and Mr. Moreno discussing plans to have her put in an institution. Heartbroken, she had gone out to find someone to help. As Del had warned, there was a man who seemed to understand her problems perfectly and wanted to help. Suddenly she was pregnant, and the man no longer cared about her problems. Incongruous though it seemed, her mother disowned her for emulating her own behavior.

Only Grandmother Perez had compassion and took her to the fields with her. When it was time for the baby's birth Carmen went to a home for unwed mothers. She kept baby Elena, espoused the Catholic faith of her grandmother, and made her home with the compassionate woman who loved her when she was rejected by her own mother.

MISSION OF A LEMON PIE

The voice on the telephone sounded vaguely familiar, but I could not place it. "I am Mrs. Mann—Rob Mann's mother—and I am sending a lemon meringue pie for your supper. I thought you'd like to know so you wouldn't prepare another dessert."

"Oh, Mrs. Mann," I protested, "you don't need to do that."

"But I want to do it," the woman insisted. "It's the least I can do. Ron and your husband have been so good to Rob. Without their tutoring, he could never have passed his math."

"They loved doing it." I laughed. "You can't imagine how many others they have done it for, too. You see, once Del had a hard time with math and a college professor helped him to become an A student. He has been trying to repay Dr. Mortimore ever since by helping others who find it tough."

"Rob will bring the pie when he comes for his lesson." Mrs. Mann closed the conversation.

With a "Thank you, we'll enjoy it," I hung the telephone on the wall hook and stood leaning against the doorpost, smiling at my own thoughts. I knew where I had heard that voice before.

It was a very rainy afternoon early in the previous winter, and we had left our old home across town to take the boys to school as we went to do the week's grocery shopping. Just around the corner and one block away from home was a street with a "yield" sign set beside a very large, sprawling mesquite tree that all but obscured the view down the intersecting street. I had rushed away from home without finishing dressing. As we approached the intersection, I was struggling to get my stockings fastened into place when I saw a purplish car, almost invisible in the haze of the rain, coming down the street toward us. Delbert paused at the yield sign but started up again; the tree and the haze blocked his view.

"Stop!" I shouted harshly, and he responded by stepping on the brakes quickly. With the slick paving, the car slowed only enough to block the path of the oncoming car. With a thunderous crash the purple LeMans hit the rear half of our Ford and flung it around to hit the front bumper of a water truck that had stopped at the other side of the intersection. Instantly the driver of the LeMans was out of her car and swearing at Del.

"Can't you see where you're going, you _____!" she screamed. "That's my sister's car . . ." and on and on.

"I'm sorry," he apologized. "I just didn't see you."

By now Del had checked us and knew that there were no serious injuries. Obviously, the single occupant of the other car was not hurt either, and the driver of the truck had hardly felt the impact on the heavy bumper.

"It's really my fault," I tried to explain. "If I had not shouted for my husband to stop, we would have cleared the intersection nicely."

The angry woman ignored my efforts and continued her tirade at Del.

"We'd better call the police," he suggested to the irate driver as he straightened from an examination of the damage. It was then that he noticed her bare arms and sleeveless dress. She certainly had not expected to be outside the car in this rain. Quickly he removed his own coat and stood in his shirt sleeves.

"Here, take this," he urged as he placed it carefully about her shoulders. "You must be cold."

Turning to me he instructed, "Take the children back to the house out of the rain." Our backdoor was just half a block and a few steps down the alley. Then he spoke again to the woman. "Would you like to come with me to call the police?" As long as I could hear them, the furious woman continued her accusations and threats.

"Did you have your seat belt fastened?" the police asked Del when they arrived. I was glad they asked him; mine was unsecured because I was still dressing. When the testimony of the truck driver coincided with Del's that he had slowed to yield but because of the tree and the rain had not seen the approaching car, no charges were made. Both cars were towed away for repairs.

"Who was she?" I asked Del when he returned home.

"Mrs. Mann," he had responded. "She was driving her sister's car. You know, her sister is the TV reporter who lives across the street from us. I guess that was why she was so upset."

I continued to smile as I moved away from the phone. "Do you suppose she's unaware that we are the same family since we have moved across town," I mused, "or is the pie part payment for the coaching in math and part apology for all the vituperation she heaped upon Del?"

FOUND IN GOD'S GOOD TIME

Del closed the slide presentation and glanced over the little group assembled in the Spicer living room. "Have you any questions?" he asked as he clicked off the projector.

"Yes!" Lillian was trembling with excitement. "How does one get to be a member of Christ's church?"

Delbert had first found the name of Lillian's husband on the official rolls of the district nearly two years before. The city in which the Spicers lived was strange to Del, and his efforts to locate the address given were unfruitful. Finally he appealed to another seventy who was familiar with the area because of his work with the Latin Americans there. Together Bob and Del found the address. Repeated visits to the house, however, always failed to produce contact with its occupants. On one such visit, Del found the house vacant. Inquiry in the neighborhood netted the information that the family had moved to Bayview, an isolated village near the seashore some thirty miles up the Gulf Coast. By making an intensive search of the area, he finally located the family in a new home on a farm outside the village.

"Would you like to go with me for a visit with the Spicers?" Del asked me after his initial visit of discovery had proved the family cordial and had resulted in an invitation for him to return. My husband believed heartily in the principle enunciated by the Christ that seventies should be sent out two by two, and when another priesthood member was not available, he frequently had me substitute.

"I would love to go!" I assured him. From experience I

knew how exciting it could be to be beside him on such a visit. The trip down palm-lined highways, past flower-decked lawns, through citrus groves and vegetable fields to the Gulf of Mexico would all be bonus.

The Spicers were waiting. Even their big German shepherd indicated his approval with wagging tail and lapping tongue.

"Will you tell Lillie about the Book of Mormon?" Willie asked as soon as the children were settled at play and the four of us were comfortably seated in the beautifully appointed living room. "I've tried, but I just haven't been 'with it' in the church for so long that I couldn't do a very good job of it."

For nearly two hours Delbert answered the questions of the eager couple. The air was charged with the Spirit of God bearing witness of the truthfulness of his testimony.

"How is it we can be so fortunate as to have them come to our house to teach us?" Lillian had never known ministers who offered this type of ministry.

"When can you come again?" the young couple asked anxiously when it was time for Willie to go to his work.

"How about next week? What days will you be available?"

The time was set, and many other visits followed. Every session was filled with excitement and expectancy as God's Spirit graced the little group. Lillie's parents came, and we were invited to join them at lunch and answer the questions they raised when the Spicers told them of the church. The family began to make the long drive to Weslaco to church when Willie's work schedule permitted.

"It's funny, isn't it, that we looked for you for so long down in Brownsville and couldn't find you?" Del remarked one day when they had shared an especially rich experience together.

"Oh, it's a good thing you didn't," Lillian assured him and smiled at the memory. "We wouldn't have listened to you then. We were so involved in the activities of the church we attended there that we wouldn't have been bothered with the truth."

Like the many visits that preceded it, Lillian's baptism was graced by the Spirit of God. The Spicer children were blessed at the same service in which she was confirmed, and the entire family glowed with happiness as it joined in the life of Christ's church.

FOILING THE "INSPECTOR"

The bell over the store door tinkled and Helga responded quickly to its summons. A large Mexican American dressed in neat perma-pressed work clothes and ten-gallon hat strode toward her from the front of the store.

"Mrs. Guzman." Helga had thought the portly gentleman who had entered the store was a customer and was surprised to hear him call her name. "I am the city inspector, and I have come to warn you that you must have those weeds between your fence and the road cut by Saturday or be fined."

"I'm sorry," Helga responded. "My husband is away at National Guard camp for two weeks. He will cut them as soon as he returns."

"You have until Saturday," the inspector spoke with finality.

"But I have the store to watch and the babies. I cannot cut the weeds on that abandoned road!" Helga was worried. "Can't it wait until Hector is home?"

"The fine is one hundred and twenty-five dollars," came the unrelenting response. One hundred and twenty-five dollars! Where would she get that much money? To cut the weeds would be impossible.

"I will be back Saturday," the inspector turned, and Helga thought she caught the glimpse of a smile that bordered on being a sneer as he walked ponderously from the building. His heavy footsteps echoed in the room, punctuating his demands.

Helga stared helplessly after the retreating figure. The meager stock scattered so skimpily over the almost bare shelves of their neighborhood store seemed to mock her as the words drummed relentlessly into her mind keeping time with the retreating footsteps. "The fine is $125.00! The fine is $125.00!" If she sold everything on the shelves, her profit would scarcely match that demand!

Just then the baby cried, and Helga could have cried with her.

She was still comforting the baby when the bell above the store tinkled again, and a familiar voice called her name. Maybe I couldn't help, but it was a relief to know that there was someone with whom she could share her consternation. The story fairly tumbled out.

"And he wouldn't even wait until Hector returned?" I was incredulous. "That's ridiculous!" I said. "Besides, where did he find any weeds around here?"

The yard beside the store and around the house was meticulously cared for—not a weed was in sight. Only neatly trimmed lawn and cultivated fruits, flowers, and garden were inside the fence that kept the children and their dog from roaming the neighborhood. I had observed it many times when Helga had taken me there to show me the progress of some particularly prized plant or shrub or to share with our family the fruits of their growing. I knew, too, that all of the mowing was done with a grass whip. The Guzmans did not own a lawn mower.

"They are the weeds outside the fence on that old dead end road to the irrigation canal that he says must be cut," Helga explained.

"Why them?" I couldn't understand. "Nobody uses that road anymore and nobody has cut weeds there for years. Why, I'll bet they're as high as my head!"

"That's why it is so hard to understand why they have to be cut by Saturday." Helga was clearly as puzzled as I.

"Well, don't you worry," I comforted my friend. "I'm sure Delbert and the boys can cut those weeds. There'll be no fine to pay." Startled as she was at the idea of a minister cutting the weeds, Helga accepted the proffered help.

Early Saturday morning Delbert loaded the mower and the boys into the car and headed for Huisache Street. The razor-sharp blade of the new mower young Steven had purchased to augment his own college fund by the proceeds of his own business made quick work of the tall, brittle weeds on the rocky roadside. The job was almost finished when the inspector drove up in his blue Volkswagen. Quite evidently he had expected to levy his fine and was obviously annoyed to find the lanky minister and his sons finishing off the weeds. Abruptly he reversed his little blue automobile and drove angrily away.

"Helga, tell me," Del requested when the work was done, "have other families in this area had to pay fines for weeds that didn't get cut in time?"

"Not always because of weeds," she replied. "Sometimes the fine is levied because a rickety fence or a tumbledown building is not repaired on time."

"Is the inspector always so anxious to get it done in a hurry?"

"Yes. Now that I think of it, he is. And he always comes when the man of the family is away working up north or in the fields at the other end of the valley."

"Do you know any of the women who have been fined? It *is* always women, isn't it?" Del was certain that his suspicions were well founded.

"Yes . . . oh, yes." Helga had not thought of that before.

"Will you get in touch with every one of them that you can find and tell them to pay their fine at the city hall next time—not to the inspector?" Del knew that no one of them could pay an entire hundred and twenty-five dollar fine in one payment so there would be installments.

Helga promised and went about delivering Del's message.

The first woman to present her fine at the city hall was met with surprise and lack of comprehension. "Your fine for not having your weeds cut?" the city clerk questioned. "Mrs. Garcia, you do not owe a fine here."

"No fine?" The woman still held her money extended across the counter as she tried to comprehend the good news. "That's what Helga's minister said, but I thought it was too good to be true."

"Helga's minister?" the clerk asked.

Mrs. Garcia explained how Helga had told her and the other women to take their money to the city hall instead of paying the inspector. "She said her minister told her to tell us," she finished thankfully.

The city clerk reported the self-appointed inspector to the police, and the police called Del for his account of the events that led to his advising Helga to instruct the women on how to handle their fines. The story made national headlines. The "inspector" never returned to levy fines among the women of the Latin-American neighborhood.

A TELEPHONE FOR THE GUZMANS

"Telephone service for your home? Of course. Please step right over to that desk and the clerk will take care of you." The receptionist of the telephone company office was gracious to the red-haired young woman who entered the office with me.

"And what may I do for you?" The receptionist turned cordially to me.

"Nothing, thank you," I replied with a smile. "I just came with Mrs. Guzman."

"Mrs. Guzz—?" the name trailed off inaudibly as the receptionist took a long look at the young woman filling out forms at the other desk.

I wandered around the room looking at pictures, studying flower arrangements, hoping that my efforts to get as near as possible to the desk at which Helga sat would be unobtrusive. I did not want to appear to be interested in the proceedings, but I did want to hear what was being said. Helga had told me of the difficulty she had experienced in getting a telephone installed in her home, and I had encouraged her to try once more. Twice in the past week burglars had attempted to break into the store portion of the house. Hector was away at National Guard camp, and there was no way for Helga to call for help if one of the children should become ill or if someone did succeed in breaking in.

It took only minutes for Helga to fill out the necessary forms requesting that the telephone be installed.

"Mrs. Guzman?" The clerk was reading from the completed application. The question in her voice evidently was there because German-born Helga didn't seem to fit the Mexican name, Guzman.

"709 East Huisache." There was no mistaking the address. It was definitely from the Mexican-American section of town.

"Mrs. Guzman." It was a statement this time. "That will be thirty-five dollars, please."

"Thirty-five dollars!" I was at Helga's side in a bound, indignation showing not only in my voice but also in my eyes.

"Thirty-five dollars!" I repeated indignantly. Helga had told me it would be like this, but I just could not believe that a reputable business like the telephone company would actually discriminate against people simply because they were of Mexican descent and lived in the section of town occupied principally by Mexican-Americans.

"Why should Mrs. Guzman have to pay thirty-five dollars for her deposit to get a phone when you charged us only seven?" I demanded of the startled clerk. Helga stood by speechlessly.

"S-s-some people move away and leave unpaid bills," stammered the clerk. She had not said "Some Mexican Americans leave unpaid bills," but the inference was obvious.

"Has Mr. Guzman left unpaid bills?" My request was firm but no longer demanding. After all, the clerk was in all probability just implementing company policy.

"No," admitted the clerk. "But . . ."

"Then why should you discriminate against the Guzmans," I interrupted, "just because some people leave unpaid bills?" I was pressing the point a bit while I pretended with the clerk that the ethnic heritage of Helga's husband had nothing to do with the exorbitant charge.

"Mrs. Guzman," the clerk turned to Helga still standing by the desk clutching the application forms in her hand. "That will be seven dollars, please," she said, obviously eager to end the embarrassing exchange.

ANDY THE MORMON PRIEST

As Andy prayed the Spirit of God settled gently over the little group that crowded into the narrow path between the two beds that constituted the furnishings of the adobe home's main room.

"We thank you, our Father, for the gifts of life you have so generously bestowed upon us." Delbert was amazed. When the portly Mexican American in whose home he had spent the evening asked him to pray with them before he left, he had gladly consented. The nature of the man's prayer, however, took Del completely by surprise.

As Andy prayed his prayer of thanksgiving, my husband mentally surveyed the circumstances from which Andy prayed. "We thank you that there has been food to eat, shelter for our family, and now that you have sent your servant to teach us the truth."

Food? A few tortillas and a pot of beans maybe. The man had not had work in weeks!

Shelter? The shack would give way to a heavy breath of air.

Del had expected the prayer of such a one to be a petition for a job, for food, for all the things the poverty-stricken family was without. Instead it was completely given to thanksgiving!

"You just can't imagine," he confessed to me, "what it was like to stand there in that crowded room and hear that thankful prayer. I know Andy has no job. They have to share their outdoor privy and single water faucet in the courtyard with ten other families. There are only two beds in that one little room for the six of them, and that tiny lean-to of a kitchen is the only place in which they can even move around."

Del had just returned from the palatial home of a rich man who thought the Lord had deserted him because the government had restricted the output of his latest oil well and the price of grapefruit had dropped before his was harvested when the telephone call had come inviting him to visit the Hernandez home. The contrast made the prayer seem all the more remarkable.

It was Andy's wife, Suzie, who had requested that Del visit them. Since she spoke very inadequate English she had asked Dominica Reyes to call for her. "Suzie wants you to come to her house to teach her children the gospel," the newly baptized member informed him.

"And how does Suzie know about the gospel?" Del needed information about the family to know its needs.

"Suzie used to belong to the church," Dominica explained, "and so did Andy. They became Mormons when there were no services in town for Spanish-speaking people. But now that the children are old enough to be baptized, Suzie wants them to know the truth."

"And Andy?" Del questioned, knowing that in Mexican-American homes the word of the husband was to be respected. "Does he want me to come?"

"Oh, yes," Dominica assured him, and the date was set. Fearing that he might not be able to converse intelligently with the Spanish-speaking couple, Del invited Elder Hector Guzman to accompany him on his first visit. Although Hector had said before they reached the house that communication with Andy would not be difficult, Del was not prepared for the flawless English with which Andy addressed him.

"Yes," he explained, "I was a member of the church, but the Mormons persuaded me to join with them here on the Mexican side of town when the Reorganization stopped having Spanish services. Suzie joined because I wanted her to, but she could not give up her belief in what she calls 'the true church.'" The big man's dark eyes sparkled as he flashed an affectionate smile at his timid, unilingual wife. It was apparent that he admired her for the strength of her convictions.

"Are you active in the Mormon faith now?" Delbert asked him.

"Oh, yes," Andy assured him. "I am a priest. I teach the priesthood class before services for the congregation on Sundays. I have to get the Sacrament ready every Sunday and help serve it. And I have the youth group on Sunday evenings."

"And it is still all right for us to teach your children in the Reorganization?" Del questioned. He was not about to break up a home if he could help it.

"Oh, yes," Andy affirmed. "I used to be a Reorganite, you know, and there are some things about the Mormon faith that bother me the same as they do Suzie."

"Perhaps you would like to return to your first baptism." Del didn't want to miss an opportunity to extend the invitation.

"I think about it sometimes," Andy confessed, "but then, I don't really know. . . ."

Del thought he knew at least a part of the reason for the

man's hesitancy. It certainly was not the language that deterred him. He had been graduated from high school and had attended college in Texas. His entire family was bilingual and numbered in its ranks educators, morticians, business people. He himself had managed a shoe store in the city until the company closed the store and wanted to transfer him out of the Valley. Fearful of leaving the familiar surroundings of the Mexican-American community, Suzie had refused to move. From that refusal until now, there had been no steady job for the family, and making a living was difficult. In the Mormon faith, however, he was a man of priesthood responsibility and position that were commensurate with his ability and training and of tremendous consequence to one without a job. He had no assurance it would be so in the Reorganization. There it would be necessary to await the call of God to priesthood, and sometimes that seemed slow in coming.

* * * * *

Though Andy's prayer had been one of thanksgiving, our prayers for the family included a petition for a job and an opportunity to live in decent housing. On Del's third trip to the home he took me along.

"I want you to know these people. Maybe you can find a way to help," he suggested.

We had lived in the border town for only a short time, and I had not been in the Mexican section except to visit the homes of active members and to pick up children for church activities. All of the members lived in simple but adequate homes; somehow it had never occurred to me that people actually lived in some of the tumbledown shacks I saw along the way.

Now as we drew to the side of the narrow street and climbed the broken steps to the rickety gate, I surveyed the grey adobe house. Crooked windows, covered by rusty screens and hung with ragged curtains and pieces of torn blanket that provided added privacy, stared from both sides of the rough, unpainted door. The dooryard, which could easily have fitted in our bathroom, was bare of vegetation.

Children's faces peered through both windows, brought there expectantly by the sound of the seventy's car for which they had been eagerly waiting. Three were beautiful, bright-eyed youngsters, happily anticipating their lesson with Del. The fourth was a mongoloid who stared solemnly at us.

As we reached the door, it flew open, powered by the hands of the eager children.

"Brother Smith! Brother Smith!" they chorused as three of them announced his arrival, then stood back shyly at the presence of the stranger with him. The mongoloid still sat on the bed on which she had climbed with the rest to see out the window. For a moment she stared suspiciously at me; then she spat violently in my direction.

"No, Noni, no!" Andy scolded the little one firmly but kindly, then apologized to his guest.

"It's all right." I smiled and assured him, "I understand." We shook hands.

Andy, too, was bursting with good news. "I have a job, Brother Smith." He could hardly wait to share his good fortune. "See, I'm a painter," and he displayed his cap and paint-splattered clothing. "God is so good to us!"

On his earlier trips to the home, Del had found that, although they were both past eight years of age, neither Aida or Junior could read well enough to understand the scriptures that he wanted to share with them. Taking a cue from a speed reading course in which he had invested, he programmed lessons for the two to accompany the gospel message he had come to share. Ardently the children tackled their study, responding equally to their reading and the gospel. Andy sat in the battered old rocker that was wedged into the area between the foot of the bed and the lean-to kitchen wall, listening intently to all that Del taught, affirming emphatically every principle of the gospel.

Soon the Hernandez family had accumulated enough money to move from their crowded shelter to a former store building divided into apartments by its resourceful owner. Now living was much easier. There was space for the children to play, a large kitchen, a sparsely furnished living room, and an ample area for their beds. They still had to share bathroom facilities, but now there were only three families to consider.

While they lived in the store building I arrived one Sunday to pick up Suzie and the children for church and found the woman hurriedly ironing a stiffly starched white shirt for her husband. "Andy preach. No shirt," she hastily explained without leaving her task. I noted her use of English. Andy declared that she understood the language well and could speak it if she were not so timid.

"Here," I volunteered, "let me iron the shirt. You get the children ready."

"I never thought I would be ironing a shirt for a Mormon preacher." I laughed as I handed the corpulent priest his shirt when it was impeccably smooth. "You had better preach an especially good sermon this morning," I teased, "with the labor of a Reorganite seventy's wife on your back!" With a parting farewell, I whisked the rest of the family into the car and off to the church of the Reorganization.

"What have you decided?" Del asked Andy when it was time for the baptismal service. "You know that Suzie wants to return to the original church. Do you want to come back with her?"

"I'm . . . I'm not sure," the man spoke hesitantly. "What did you say I would have to do?"

"Well, Suzie is going to make a statement to the congregation telling of her baptism in the Mormon church and of her desire to return to the Reorganization because she believes it to be the true church. Of course, her statement will be translated into English so the English-speaking members will understand. Then the branch president will ask the members of the congregation if they will accept her in full fellowship on her original baptism. If they vote 'yes'—and I'm sure they will—she will be declared fully restored to membership and will join with the rest of us in receiving the sacrament of the Lord's Supper.

"You could make your own statement saying just what you want to say, and receive the vote of the people along with her if you feel that it is the right thing to do."

"I do think it is the right thing to do," Andy said resolutely. "I will be there with Suzie and the children."

When the baptismal day arrived, however, Andy was called to a special duty in the Mormon church. He did not even witness the baptism of his children nor Suzie's return to the faith she held dear.

Soon the family moved again. Andy was painting steadily now with a Mormon brother who also found them their new home across the street from his own. The sprawling structure was old but comfortable. Bright asphalt shingles covered the exterior of the house, giving it some insulation from the burning Valley sun. There was modern plumbing all their own. And the countryish yard included a generous rock pile and an old shed just meant to suit the fancies of the children at play.

Good times were short-lived for the Hernandez family, however. Here Andy had his first stroke, although it was really never diagnosed as such. He was so ill that he could no longer paint. He did not complain, but when we stopped by after dark and found candlelight because the electricity had been cut off by the city, our bishop's agent came in with oblation funds, paid the rent and the utility bills, and saw to it that there was food.

Christmas came while Andy was still ill, and the church people saw to it that there was ample for celebration.

"Just look!" Andy shook his head as though he was still unable to believe it when he showed us the tree, the gifts, and recounted the food they had had. We had been out of the Valley during the holiday and so had not had a part in the festivities. Cruz Silva had acted for the church in her capacity as Friendly Visitor, coordinating the activity. "They even came and sang carols for us." Tears shimmered in the sick man's eyes, and he bit his lip to stop its quivering as he recalled the experience. "God is so good to us!" the thankful man reaffirmed.

The Hernandez family's next move was into a white, two-bedroom cottage that had a large living room with a picture window overlooking a beautiful grassy lawn enclosed by a neat picket fence. From the kitchen sink, Suzie could keep an eye on the little ones as they played in the shady backyard. There was garden space large enough to provide vegetables and fruits in quantity once they could get it into production.

Andy's new job was that of manager of a large filling station at the eastern confluence of the federal highway with the major thoroughfare through the city. The big man fit into his managerial position with ease. His shoe store experience had helped him get the job. This was the family's first return to a prospect of real prosperity since Suzie's refusal to move with the store.

But again prosperity for the Hernandezes was short-lived. Help was hard to get at the wages allowed by the oil company, and Andy found himself working longer and longer hours. Often it was insufferably hot, and the snack foods and carbonated beverages so readily available tasted good! Andy began to add to his already excessive weight. One day he fell at work and had to be taken home. In a few hours he had recovered and was back on the job.

The next time he fell, he had to be taken to the hospital. This stroke was more severe and could be readily diagnosed. His left leg and arm were paralyzed, and he was faced with a long period of recuperation without funds.

"Where are the employment benefits? Is there no insurance in such a large oil company?" Del inquired.

"None," Andy answered with resignation. "It seems that is why they make men like me managers. That way they don't have to provide us with employee benefits."

"Can you get along without assistance?" Del was leaving the city for an extended missionary trip and he was concerned.

"Oh, yes. We'll make it," Andy assured him with a crooked smile. The muscles of his face were affected, too. "I'll be back at work soon."

NO FOOD IN THE HOUSE

Andy was not at work soon. Days went by, then weeks. He was better, but there was no longer a managership awaiting his recovery, and he was not well enough to get a new job.

One Sunday evening there was a social event at the church, complete with punch and cookies. Andy appeared at the church with three of the children in time for the refreshments. I was presiding at the punch bowl when the children came in. Shyly they approached the table in their turn. I noted the look in their eyes and the way they consumed the food hungrily. Quietly I slipped away from my post at the table and invited the children to return. This time I filled their plates and urged them to eat all they wanted.

"Delbert, I think I had better get down to the Hernandez house and see what's going on," I confided to my husband when we were home. "It isn't like Andy to bring the children to the church just for refreshments, and those children were hungry!"

"Shall we go before I leave town in the morning?" Del hesitated a little. His trip the next day was an urgent one.

"No," I assured him, "you just won't have time. I'll go after you leave."

Del had barely pulled away when I began to gather things to take to the Hernandez home. On the table I spotted the bag of grapes I had prepared for him to munch as he drove (munching fruit helped relieve the monotony of many miles of driving, and he was less likely to fall asleep at the wheel). Hastily I grabbed them up and ran out the door after my husband, but it was too late. He was already out of sight.

Maybe the children would enjoy them, I thought, and added the grapes to the loaf of homemade bread and stick of margarine I had just placed in another bag.

The mile or so walk in the beautiful autumn morning was invigorating. Already winter visitors were gathering in the trailer courts, refurbishing the mobile homes they had left behind when they had gone north for the summer. The fragrance of orange blossoms had given way to the ripening fruit on the gnarled old trees left behind when housing encroached on the orchards that once filled the area. Voices of happy children at recess added still another pleasant note as I passed the school grounds on my way.

Suzie's faint call, "Come in," answered my knock. The

voice sounded tired, or muffled, or far away. I hesitated a moment, reluctant to enter without being admitted to the home but feeling that I should enter, for all was not well. Slowly I opened the screen door and peered into the room. On the single bed that served as a living room couch Suzie lay quietly, making no effort to rise to greet me. Lusterless eyes stared wearily from her thin face.

"What's the matter, Suzie?" I rushed to her side.

"Seeek!" It was an effort for the woman to talk.

"Where's Andy?" I looked around the room and listened for the sound of activity. Suzie gestured feebly toward the kitchen, and I ran to see what I would find there.

The kitchen was not as clean as the living room. A large laundry tub stood on a stool just inside the door. In it a scrub board was braced against a mass of soured laundry abandoned halfway through the wash. It must have been untouched for days. Dirty dishes in the sink showed a similar abandonment. On the table were four glasses, each with just a hint of chocolate coloring.

"Andy! Andy!" I called sharply, beginning to panic as I envisioned some of the things that might have happened. With relief I heard his voice from the backyard.

Walking slowly and leaning heavily on his cane, he moved painfully toward the house swinging his left leg awkwardly, his left arm dangling. Noni and Jupiter were with him.

"Andy, what has happened? What is wrong with Suzie?" I questioned urgently.

"Oh, Sister Smith, I'm so glad you are here!" he said gratefully as he dragged himself inside the back door and fell into the chair just inside the kitchen.

"Why didn't you tell us last night that you needed us?" I scolded.

"I wanted to, but . . ." he didn't try to explain.

"How long has Suzie been sick?"

"I don't know. All week I guess. She gave her food to the children."

"You mean she hasn't eaten for a week?" I was horrified.

"More than a week," Andy corrected wearily. "She got so weak she couldn't finish the washing and I couldn't . . ." He stared helplessly at his impotent hand and crippled foot. I wondered how he got the children to the church the night before. He must have asked someone to bring them.

"It wasn't so bad for me," he went on. "The doctor is giving me medicine to keep me from feeling hunger while I take off this extra weight, and I couldn't get very hungry without working anyway."

"And the children?" I knew now why Andy had made the effort to get them to the church.

"All they have had since Friday was what they ate at the church last night—except Suzie saved enough dry milk to make a glass of chocolate milk for them this morning. They divided it between the four of them before Junior and Aida went to school."

"Oh, Andy!" I said reproachfully as I gathered the little ones to me and hurried them to the table where I cut the bread, buttered it, and gave it to them to eat. "Why didn't you let us know?"

Hearing the commotion, Suzie arose from the couch and staggered into the kitchen.

"Here," I pressed a slice of the buttered bread into her hands along with a bunch of the grapes.

"Los Niños," the anxious mother whispered, extending the food toward the little ones eating ravenously at the table.

"There is plenty for the children. Eat it, Suzie!" I commanded brusquely, and turned away to hide the tears that flowed down my cheeks. The bread, butter, and grapes were such a meager offering! Why had I not brought more? If only I had checked earlier—even last night!

Andy, too, accepted a small portion of the food, and it was gone quickly.

"Make a list of the groceries you need," I urged him, "and I'll go get them."

"Could you?" There was relief in his voice. "I'll pay you for them as soon as I get work."

"Aren't you getting help from welfare?" I did not want to pry, but this state of affairs was intolerable.

"No," Andy responded, "but I will be back to work soon."

"This time, Andy, we're not waiting for work," I vowed. "Is it all right with you if I go make arrangements for Aida and Junior to have free lunches at the school cafeteria? They're entitled to them, you know."

Receiving his nod of approval, I continued. "Will you go with me to the welfare office to get help from there?"

"If you think it's all right. . . ." He was still reluctant to accept any kind of charity.

"That's what it's for!" I was positive in the pronouncement. "I'll go make the appointment right now and get those groceries."

"I'll pay you back," Andy affirmed again.

This time I ran through the late morning hush intent only on getting food for the family, especially for Junior and Aida who had had nothing since the quarter glass of chocolate milk for breakfast. At school it took only minutes to apprise the principal of the children's need and make arrangements for their daily lunches, beginning in minutes from the time of my visit to the office. Straight from the office, I hurried to the music room where I knocked on the door and spoke to another seventy's wife who taught there.

"Could I borrow your car, Jessie?" I asked. "I need to run an errand for the Hernandez family," and I briefly told my friend of their plight. The keys to her car were soon in my possession. "Don't worry if you aren't back by the time school is out," she said. "I can walk home if you need the car."

Back from grocery shopping, I stopped by our own pantry and added a few items not on the list that I knew were needed to provide well balanced meals until needed funds were forthcoming. Then, returning to the cottage I exchanged groceries for dirty laundry, stayed long enough to tidy up the kitchen, help fix a meal for the family, and arrange for the trip to the welfare office at three. "I told them we had to see them today because it is an emergency," I said.

Inadequate though they were, the welfare funds kept the family from starving. Suzie regained her strength, and Andy began slowly to recover.

ANDY NEVER QUITE RETURNS

One day I answered the doorbell to find Suzie and three of the children standing on the broad veranda that stretched the full width of the sturdy old brick house. It was noon and we were just sitting down to a leftover meal of rice and beans.

"Come, join us," I urged, sorry that the food would be such a repetition of what they would have at home. Suzie and the children seemed not to mind. When the meal was finished, she announced, "Go get Andy."

"Where's Andy?" I questioned in surprise.

"Beside the road," Junior explained. "He got tired and could not walk all the way."

"You mean," I asked incredulously, "we let him sit beside the road in this hot sun while we ate lunch?"

Suzie nodded.

"And Jupiter?" I had thought the two were at home together.

"He is with him," Aida said precisely, then ducked her head and giggled at my consternation.

"Why didn't you tell me?" I would never learn to ask the right questions at the right time, it seemed.

"No help. No car." Suzie shrugged.

"I know Delbert has the car, but I could borrow one to go get him!" In my concern my voice sounded harsh and impatient. I was worried that Andy's inability to walk all of the way might be due to something more serious than exhaustion. "Go find him. See that he's all right," I commanded. "I'll run to the school and borrow Sister Weldon's car and come for him."

Andy was just tired and gratefully accepted both the ride and the lunch of rewarmed beans and rice.

"I just had to tell you," Andy revealed the purpose of the long walk when the meal was finished. "Suzie's father came to me last night."

"Suzie's father?" I was puzzled. I knew that Suzie had tried to get her mother across the border from Mexico, but I had never heard anyone mention her father.

"The old man has been dead a lot of years now," Andy explained, "but he came to me last night and told me to go to Leonidas—that's Suzie's birthplace in Mexico—and teach Suzie's people about the Christ."

"Did he tell you what to teach?" I remembered Andy's wish to ask the Christ which church was His.

"I asked him, and he answered, irritated because he

thought I ought to know, 'Why the Reorganization, of course'!"

"That was all?"

"Yes, really. The old man kept telling me over and over to do it, so I could never forget it. I tried to get him to go away and let me sleep, but he wouldn't for a long time."

"So now you know!"

But Andy just couldn't bring himself to leave his place of honor and responsibility among the Mormons.

"I missed being ordained an elder by forty-nine dollars," he announced one day when we were visiting.

"How do you mean, forty-nine dollars?" Del was puzzled by his statement.

"You know how hard up we were all last year when I was sick," he recounted. "Well, I didn't pay forty-nine dollars of my tithing, so I couldn't be ordained an elder."

"Andy, you ought to follow Suzie's father's advice," Del chided him gently. "Don't you know that according to scripture you should pay a tenth of your increase—not of your income—in tithing? Why, in the Reorganization you could never have *owed* forty-nine dollars tithing last year. How can your church demand a tenth of your welfare check when it barely keeps you from starving?"

* * * * *

When Andy could use his arm almost normally—although his foot still dragged a bit when he was tired—welfare personnel began to talk rehabilitation. We provided transportation and counsel in connection with numerous agencies involved until the transfer was made, and Andy enrolled in barber school to train for a new career.

There was some delay in processing the necessary papers, resulting in an accumulation of funds that arrived in one sizable compensation check for the family. "I want to pay you for the groceries," Andy announced one day when he appeared at our door.

"You don't need to do that," I insisted, "certainly not until you are back at work."

"But I want to pay you," the grateful man persisted. "Didn't you say it was twelve dollars?"

"Wait a minute," I said, handing him the store tape which I had kept in my purse awaiting this minute. "It was exactly eleven dollars and ninety-seven cents."

Surprised and pleased, Andy protested, "That wasn't necessary."

"Business is business," I observed with a smile. "I wanted you to know I wasn't cheating you!" Both of us knew what I really meant was that I wanted him to know I trusted him.

Barber school was a highly successful venture for Andy. Getting established in the profession took some time, however, and there was still a period of privation ahead for the family.

One day a telephone call came from the barbershop in which Andy had begun his career. "Suzie is sick. Could you take her to the doctor?" Andy requested. "Please come by for me. I think I should go along."

Assuming it to be a routine errand, I took the car leaving Del to work in his office. I was shocked to find the sick woman, hemorrhaging severely, lying semiconscious in her blood-stained bed.

"How long has this been going on?" My concern showed in my voice.

"Eleven days now," Andy replied.

"Eleven days!" I exclaimed. This was nearly as bad as the time without food. "Why *didn't* you tell us?"

"We thought every day it would surely stop." Andy was worried, too.

If only Delbert was along! But to get him would take

time, and there seemed need for haste in this situation. Hurriedly I pulled the car as close to the front door as possible. Between us we half carried the suffering woman and laid her on a bed of pillows and quilts in the back seat of the car. She fainted just as we reached the car door. Again she fainted on the way from the car into the examining room. Sensing the seriousness of the situation, the doctor ordered immediate hospitalization, beginning with transfusions in the emergency room.

Five units of blood were required before Suzie regained her strength. The blood could be paid for with one hundred and fifty dollars or ten units of blood for the bank. It would take months to accumulate that kind of money in addition to the hospital and doctor bills . . . and there was not enough family this side of the border to fill the replacement order.

"Don't worry," Del assured the family, "I'm sure the Saints will be glad to replenish the blood bank."

Delbert was out of town again by the time Suzie was strong enough for the surgery the doctors felt was necessary to restore her to health. Other elders offered prayers in her behalf at her bedside before the operation began. I sat holding her hand as she drifted off to oblivion after the preliminary drugs were given, assuring her that that which was about to be done would not cause Andy to love her the less.

On the Sunday following the surgery, the pastor had me make the announcement about the need for blood to replace that used for Suzie. "Only those over eighteen and younger than sixty years will be accepted as donors." I relayed the information as I informed the group of the hours for giving and other details. When the service was finished, there were numerous volunteers. Some who were too old to give blood insisted on giving the equivalent in money. When the donations were totaled, there was no expenditure to be made for the blood, and the doctor's bill was presented to the hard-pressed barber marked, "Paid in full."

"I thought the office girl said the doctor would charge fifty dollars." I approached Andy with the canceled bill.

"That's what she said," Andy affirmed.

"Then how did it get to be fifty-five?" I questioned the figure on the receipt.

"Oh, it has been more than a month," Andy explained. "Ten percent is added to the bill if it is not paid in a month."

"Ten percent a month!" I could hardly believe it. Mentally I made a note to see the doctor. Perhaps there would be some way to stop that kind of injustice to the poor!

Word had come from the world church that Delbert must move to another area of ministry, however, and the inequity in billing charges was never pursued. Likewise Andy's new determination to return to the Reorganization was left for him to arrange with others. However, the next stroke took his life. His return was never effected.

ALL THE DIFFERENCE IN THE WORLD

The class of appointee ministers and their wives was suddenly interrupted by the entry of a dozen or more people, the entourage of the director of the School of the Restoration. "These are Graceland's elite!" the director introduced the group touring the church institutions in preparation for their summer's work as institutional representatives at camps and conferences. We exchanged quick glances, then fastened our gazes on the oldest couple among the Gracelanders. There was time only for a quick wave of recognition, a smile of commendation, and the visitors were whisked on their way.

Class resumed, but I scarcely heard the instructor. "Graceland's elite!" The appellation kept singing through my consciousness. "Graceland's elite!" What a difference the gospel makes!

It had been nearly twenty years since Patriarch James Thomas, nonresident pastor of the area to which we were assigned, had called our attention to Edythe's name on the rolls. "Husband—nonmember," the record indicated. "Children—three."

"Brother Jake and Brad will be in the area," the patriarch suggested. "Why don't we ask them to drop in and see what the prospects are for you to follow up with some ministry to try to unite that home?"

The report back was far from encouraging. "The wife seems interested," the elders reported, "but, oh, that man! Religion is the farthest thing from his mind! He's a truck driver and is often gone from home. When he is there, he is rough with his family—doesn't seem to notice that they are living in poverty. He smokes, drinks, gambles, swears. You name it. He does it. Only a miracle could change him!"

"Isn't that what the gospel is for—to perform miracles?"

Del could not get the family off his mind.

Soon there was word that the Baldwins had moved into the city. We drove to the oldest part of town to visit them at their new address. Trash littered the yards and crept into the doorways and onto the streets. Gaping holes stared from the vacant houses where vandals had carried out their window-smashing ritual. Crude patches, sometimes of cardboard, sometimes of jagged glass, sometimes of rags, were used to keep out the snow, rain, and chill from the houses now inhabited. For most of the houses, paint was just a memory. Rattletrap cars parked in front of many homes bespoke the struggle of the family inside. The smell of poverty hung in the air.

The Baldwins' house was like the rest, crowded close to the neighbors. Had it not been for a decrepit fence separating them, even a child could easily have jumped from one porch to another.

The interior of the house was bleak and ugly as the outside. Bare, rough floors bore the marks of many careless families. The smoky drabness of the walls was broken only by holes in the plaster and an occasional picture retrieved from a calendar, some of questionable vintage. Bare light bulbs sparsely illuminated the meager furnishings of the cheerless home.

But we were not the first to visit the Baldwins. A young priest, Doyle Sundell, had first learned of the family's move to the city and called on them. Reminiscences of their early youth together in another state reminded Edythe of the joys the church had brought to her and kindled a desire for her children to have some of the same privileges. Already they had made plans to attend church with the Sundells.

Soon Del and the young priest were conducting cottage meetings in the home. Before long Walter asked for baptism.

"Is it all right if Doyle is the one who officiates?" Del inquired. "As a priest he has the authority to baptize you in water. I have the authority to baptize you with the Holy Spirit. If it is all right with you, I would like for both of us to have a part in your entry into the kingdom of God."

Walter agreed quickly and gladly. When Doyle received the news, he was elated. And as Del and Brother Thomas prayed for the confirming ministry of the Holy Spirit, each received the assurance that Walter would one day serve in God's priesthood.

Shortly after his baptism, Walter had an opportunity for a better job in another city. This time the family moved into an inexpensive but new area of the city where they purchased a partially constructed house on a lot adequate for both a yard and a garden. Nearly a year passed before we heard from them again.

It was a beautiful Sunday morning when the Baldwins arrived back in the city to attend church—neat, clean, well-dressed, and radiant.

"Can you have lunch with us?" I asked eagerly. Del was ministering out of town, as was so often the case, but I was delighted to see the family and eager to learn what was transpiring in their lives. The Baldwins could hardly wait to share their good news.

On the way home from church, everyone talked joyfully. Walter had been called and ordained to the priesthood and was serving as pastor of the junior church in a large congregation in his new area.

"Has the church made a difference in your life?" I asked on the way home.

"All the difference in the world!" Walter replied fervently.

Arrival at our house and the necessity to prepare the meal cut short the conversation.

Two days later there was a letter in the mail from Walter.

Dear Mildred,

I have been thinking of that question you asked me on the way home from church. If you don't recall it, here it is again. You asked me if I could see any difference in my life since I joined the church.

The answer I gave then does not satisfy me so I am going to try to put some of the changes in my life on paper for you.

I have new desires and a new outlook on life. Now I don't look to get more out of life than I put into it. I seem to have a deeper sense of responsibility, not only toward myself and my family but toward the people around me. I feel as though I have a purpose in life. All my thinking has changed. I have the desire to overcome my weaknesses and fears.

I have no desire for "the way of the world" any more, such as the craving for tobacco, alcohol, and cards that I used to have. My desires for alcohol had started to change a few years before I joined the church. I believe that was God's influence showing in my life then.

I had a feeling from the first time Edythe told me about this church that it was the church I had been looking for. The belief is what I always thought a church should have. I kept all of this from my wife.

This letter has even created a change in me, for I feel now as though a big load has been taken off my shoulders.

I can also see that there are still a lot of changes to be made, but I know that with God's help I will be able to make them.

Now that I have this letter finished, I feel as if I have answered your question.

May God bless you.
Yours truly,
Walter C. Baldwin

Years passed. Our paths and the Baldwins' crossed and recrossed. I smiled as I remembered the Cub Scouts Edythe had "mothered" in our home. I wept at the trauma of the Baldwins' oldest son who didn't hear very well and whose body just refused to keep pace with others of his age. I remembered joyfully Jeanie's first story. She had written it for her Light of Life award, and we had insisted that she submit it to *Stepping Stones* for publication. I remembered, too, the many stories that followed in the church publications both from Jeanie and her mother, some of which mirrored the life of our own family. I remembered the births of three other Baldwin children, and thankfully recalled the day young George knelt in the garden beside a raging grass fire and prayed for the Lord to put it out when all of the family's concerted efforts had failed to halt its progress toward their home; and the Lord promptly answered his prayer.

Now Walter was a part of the custodial staff of Graceland College. Bill, whose body refused to grow in his early teens, and whose faulty hearing made him seem a bit strange to his peers, had received all of the honors available in high school mathematics, had been named to *Who's Who in American Colleges* for his achievements in that educational level, and now had his own brass plaque on a Graceland office door. "Mr. William Baldwin," I had read on our last visit there and almost burst with thankfulness.

Jeanie had long since been graduated from Graceland, given of her time in the Older Youth Corps, taught school in an area where another seventy had requested that she teach so she could be available to assist with the work of the Lord among the culturally deprived whose needs she understood so well. Edythe, too, had been graduated by Graceland and was well into her new career as an elementary teacher. The younger members of the family were all in school.

With Edythe's degree completed, the Baldwins had decided to give a summer to publicizing the institutions of the Church of Jesus Christ which for them had made "all the difference in the world!"